THE
OFF-ROAD
RACING BOOK

THE OFF-ROAD RACING BOOK

Alan Harman

ARGUS BOOKS

Argus Books
Argus House
Boundary Way
Hemel Hempstead
Hertfordshire HP2 7ST
England

First published by Argus Books 1990

Publisher's Note
The word 'buggy' has been changed to 'car' throughout the text for international publishing purposes.

ISBN 0 85242 994 0

Phototypesetting by The Works, Exeter, Devon. EX4 3LS, England.
Printed and bound in Great Britain by Dotesios Printers Ltd, Trowbridge, Wilts.

CONTENTS

1 INTRODUCTION

The hobby of radio controlled off-road model cars has grown in the last ten years from a small number of Japanese 'fun' cars to back garden runner to the international racing scene driver.

In the early years Tamiya — the largest manufacturer of radio controlled cars — produced two 1:12th scale cars which opened the door of radio controlled cars to everyone, as the cars could be run on almost any surface and did not require a specially-built circuit. This soon led to the car explosion and the flood of kits available today, ranging from simple Ready to Run (RTR) cars to sophisticated Four-Wheel Drive (4WD) race vehicles and the 1:8th scale Internal Combustion (IC) powered Rallycross cars.

The British-made Schumacher 'CAT' has proven to be one of the world's best off-road cars.

ELECTRIC OR ENGINE POWER?

The electric car boom has come mainly from Japan, whereas the racing side of Rallycross (1:8th scale IC) has stemmed mainly from Europe, with a number of manufacturers vying for the Rallycross market. Recently, though, the Japanese have added their unquestionable talents in kit production and quality to the Rallycross market, making the 1:8th scene more easily available to the average radio controlled car enthusiasts.

Tamiya's Grasshopper — the most popular R/C car in the world.

WHERE TO START?

There are two forms of off-road car power — internal combustion and electric. Even with the recent intervention of the Japanese manufacturers, IC cars do require greater skills in building, running and maintenance than their electric-powered brothers — not to mention their extra cost.

By far the most popular starting model is a 1:10th electric-powered car. These kits generally have excellent instructions and very high build quality.

Schumacher's reasonably priced 2WD car — the Topcat.

WHAT'S AVAILABLE?

On the 1:10th car side, there is an enormous range from which to choose. If you prefer, there is no need to enter into kit building at all, as both Tamiya and Kyosho offer Ready to Run cars which come with a fully completed car and radio system together in one box — all that is required is the fitting of the Ni-cad batteries and you're off! These cars, of course, have a limited speed, and have the drawback of taking four hours to charge, but they still offer an excellent introduction to car racing.

Next in line is the starter kit range. The Tamiya Grasshopper II leads the way here, and is the most popular radio controlled car ever. This car comes with a 380 motor (the smaller of the two sizes available) and is constructed with a simple two-wheel drive system and neat but simple suspension.

Next is a variation on the two-wheel drive theme — the Astute from Tamiya or Ultima from Kyosho are both more advanced forms of the two-wheel drive chassis. These kits come complete (with motor and speed controller) but still require a radio control system. Both these kits have 540 motors (the standard electric size) and have oil-filled shocks, independent suspension and are generally purpose-built to go quickly.

The main change to the next stage is the addition of four-wheel drive. This, again, is offered in a variety of prices and levels, from simple chassis to advanced racing machines, available with four-wheel belt drive and complicated turnable suspension, and is aimed mainly at the racing end of off-road car racing.

The Kyosho Burns has made Rallycross easy with its excellent instructions and build quality.

Ready for fun! — a quick drive car from Tamiya.

American 2WD car, the RC10, in action.

IN AT THE DEEP END

If you decide that the Internal Combustion 1:8th Rallycross class is the car you wish to own, there are a number of extra factors you need to take into account. Apart from the extra cost of a 1:8th car, you also have to buy an engine, suitable radio, starter and 2 volt battery. As well as this, fuel and a 12 volt battery are the minimum requirements to run a 1:8th car.

There are fewer areas in which a 1:8th car can be run, as noise and safety must be taken into account — public annoyance is not acceptable. With this in mind, there are also fewer clubs running 1:8th, although this should not put you off what must be considered the most exciting form of car racing.

Nowadays the IC car class consists mainly of Japanese-produced, four-wheel drive cars. The present-day kits are relatively easy to build and give high levels of reliability and build quality. There certainly are still a large number of European-built cars, but these generally do not have the built-in Japanese high quality of product and building instructions. All of these kits feature alloy chassis shaft-drive systems and are normally suspended by oil-filled coil over dampers.

Apart from the 1:8th car class, a new less sophisticated area has recently started to prove popular. Simple two-wheel drive, pull-start Rallycross cars are now available, which use the same IC engines but cut out the starting problems with a clever pull-start recoil system. These kits are reasonably priced and should be considered as an introduction to 1:8th Rallycross racing.

Smooth bodyshell lines produced on this Tamiya 2WD Astute.

2 THINK ELECTRIC

Well, if you've decided that an electric-powered 1:10th scale off-road car is where you are going to start, then you've probably made a wise decision. Fun is what it's all about and the building and running of an electric car is certianly that. Now you have an enormous range of cars to choose from, so let's look at a car's main parts so that you may choose your model.

All 1:10th off-road cars are designed for just that — off-road!! The cars feature a large amount of ground clearance to allow the wheels to keep in contact with the ground and the chassis away from the surface over which the car is moving.

The cars are rugged, and are designed and built from materials which are light yet tough, allowing the usual punishment to be dished out without breakages.

All 1:10th cars centre around the chassis. This can be in various forms. Most 'economy' type cars feature an injection moulded plastic 'tub'. This is cheap to produce in high numbers, tough due to the ribs and sections of the tub and also very light, yet gives a solid mounting for the drive system, suspension and the radio/battery components.

Some of the more complicated cars feature a dual fibre glass box chassis. This features a bottom flat plate of glass fibre to which components are bolted; then a second layer is bolted on top to form a 'box' which gives a very strong section in which all the components can be contained.

To form this rigidity, you can also use more high tech, although expensive, materials which form just one plate. Carbon fibre is often used at the top of the car range to form a single chassis plate which, due to the properties of carbon, gives a strong stiff chassis, but at a price. Various alloys of aluminium are also used in most chassis as supports or mounts — this is, of course, light, strong and reasonably cheap.

One of the most successful cars ever — The Associated RC10.

THE UPS AND DOWNS

To the chassis is fitted the suspension. The idea of the suspension is that the car can follow the undulations of the ground and still keep in contact with the surface, thereby allowing the wheels to drive and the car to move forward.

There are various forms of suspension available. On the low-cost starter area of 1:10th cars, a solid rear axle which also includes the motor is widely used. This means that the whole rear axle and motor are suspended from the chassis, which allows an amount of movement although it is not ideal for off-road use.

The front end of these cars usually features independent, single arm suspension. This allows the car to soak up the bumps but does have some disadvantages, in that the wheels can end up at various angles to the surface. Both the front and rear of these cars, as in the Tamiya Grasshopper, are sprung only with coil springs and do not feature oil-filled dampers. This system is excellent for this level of car but, as will be explained later, it is a very simple system compared to the top-of-the-range cars.

The next stage of suspension features fully-independent movement for all four wheels. This, of course, requires a system for taking the drive to the wheels in a flexible way, but more of that later.

Independent suspension comes under two main headings — trailing arm and double wishbone parallelogram. The first, and the least used, consists of a suspension arm pivoting across the width of the car's chassis so that the bumps hit the arm from the front of the pivot point.

This system is very good at soaking up undulations, but is limited in the amount of adjustment that can be made.

Racing action form the 1:10th Off-Road World Championships.

KEEP INDEPENDENT

By far the most widely used of all suspension systems in 1:10th cars is the independent method. This system allows for changes to be made easily in camber and castor — two important areas for tuning the handling of a car. Basically, the system uses a main arm pivoting from low down in the chassis, and to the end of this arm is fixed the hub (this holds the wheel). The top of the hub is then controlled with a further arm fixed to the top of the chassis. The mounting points on the chassis and hub can then be easily altered, allowing for various angles of camber and castor. This may all sound quite complicated but is in practice quite simple. Later, the 'how to' and 'why' of castor and camber alteration will be explained, but, when choosing a kit, it is important to know whether the suspension is adjustable.

Ready-built Hirobo — only requires radio control to be fitted.

PUTTING A DAMPER ON IT

The movement of the suspension on cars is controlled in various ways. On the simple chassised cars, a coil spring is used to keep the car sprung-up from the ground. This works well and allows the cars to be driven across most types of terrain. However, a problem with this is that, from bump to bump, the car often starts to leap, as the spring uncoils quickly after being squashed up from hitting a bump. This unspringing unbalances the car and impedes its handling. What is required, and is fitted on the more sophisticated cars, is an oil damper. The spring is fitted over the damper, and the compression and spring-back of the spring is controlled by oil in the damping moving part or piston. Basically, the spring is slowed down, stopping rebound and keeping the wheels of the car in contact with the ground. Whether a kit includes oil-filled dampers is important, as these are often expensive extras which are almost vital for running over bumpy ground.

ELECTRIC MOTORS

Some sort of motor is included in all kits, except the very top-of-the-range racing vehicles. In the lower-priced, reduced specification kits, a 380 motor is fitted (380 refers to the size and therefore the power). Apart from these kits, the rest use the standard-sized 540 motor which is larger than the 380 and is more powerful.

In kits supplied with motors, a method of controlling the speed is also included. This is usually in the form of a mechanical speed controller which consists of three forward speeds and reverse, operated by the servo (part of the radio control system). They are generally robust and are perfectly adequate for the job, although more advanced, non-mechanical electronic speed controllers are available for the racing end of the market.

Most cars feature some system of changing the gear ratio used to drive the car. This is similar to a gearbox in real cars but the difference is that a single 'gear' is chosen and the car runs on this one gear only. Obviously, more speed gives less running time from the battery, and vice versa, so gear ratios can be selected to 'tune' the car to run for a certain period of time at a certain speed. Normally, kits include two ratios in the box — a high and low setting — although further alternatives are normally available.

A quick drive Tamiya Pumpkin — as it comes.

MAIN CHOICE

Your main decision will be whether to have a four-wheel drive or two-wheel drive car.

Two-wheel drive cars are generally cheaper, as they have less parts. They are slightly more difficult to drive, as the cars have less grip, but can be more fun, as long slides and wheel spin often occur more with two-wheel drive than four. Maintenance is also reduced, as are wear rates and therefore running costs.

Four-wheel drive is by far the most popular for racing. The cars are still simple in construction, well-designed and give massively increased grip and speed over the two-wheel drive cars.

Losi JRX2 front suspension is tough and well designed.

Today's 1:10th cars have excellent suspension to soak up the bumps.

Carbon chassis is stiff yet very light.

Schumacher main gear fitted to a 4WD Procat.

DRIVE SYSTEMS

Two-wheel drive cars have a very simple drive system. All cars are gear-driven from the motor to the main gear; the drive is then further passed to the differential via more gears or a drive toothed belt. The differential — either geared or ball type — then passes the drive to the wheels via the drive shafts. The operation is basically the same on four-wheel drive cars, except that the drive is taken to the front wheels via shafts or toothed belts. The majority of cars use shafts, although belts are accepted as the most efficient system to transfer the power from one end of the chassis to the other.

Once the power is at the diffs, the drive shaft's job is to drive the wheel. This is done through a plastic or steel universal joint and ball pin system. Of course the lighter the drive system, the better, as less power is used up in the transfer process.

Wheels and tyres play a large part in the performance of any car. Hundreds of different tyres are available for a variety of surfaces — for grass, pinspikes; for sand, ribs; and for tarmac, hard-wearing blocks. Tyres are often the first modification to any car and most kits come with suitable tyres as standard.

Tamiya's Astute has adjustable suspension for tuning.

UP ON TOP

What probably makes most people choose one car rather than another is the look of its bodyshell.

Two main materials are used. ABS is a hard plastic which is injection moulded and produces highly-detailed, but brittle, bodyshells. This can be easily painted with car sprays on the surface and made to look great with self-adhesive stickers.

Lexan is a super, tough, clear plastic which is widely used. It is vacuum formed and, when cooled down, is incredibly strong. These lexan shells are painted on the inside which can be tricky, but they stop scratching during use as the paint is protected inside the car.

Off-road cars are often run through mud and water, so it's important to see if the car is protected with an undertray. This seals to the body and protects the electronics and internals of the car.

Some kits come with wings — these often improve the look of the car and the handling — and it is worth checking to see if the kit you like has a wing or whether one can be easily fitted at a later date. Don't forget, though, that lexan requires special paint that 'bonds' to the plastic. As kits are not supplied with paint, don't forget the added cost.

What you must remember is that kits do not come with batteries, chargers or radio control equipment so you'll have to pay more than the price of the kit. Don't forget to budget for a handful of spares, and even two battery packs.

3 INTERNAL COMBUSTION RALLYCROSS CARS

The least supported and least popular area of radio controlled cars is the internal combustion-powered 1:8th Rallycross class. The low popularity of this class in no way derives from the lack of enjoyment, as the Rallycross cars, with their high power-to-weight ratio and speed, must rate as the most exciting form of cars to drive and watch. The main drawback in the past has been their high cost and the general difficulty in owning and running the car, due to the extra problems in making an IC engine run reliably and for long periods of time.

Nowadays, there are three main ways to start out in Rallycross.

1:10th SCALE

At the bottom end of the market is the easiest form of IC car available. Almost-ready-to-run 1:10th scale cars are now available, which use many of the 1:10th scale electric car chassis components. These are then coupled up to a simple 2.00 cc 0.10 cu. in. IC motor with a recoil pull-start system. These cars are of extremely high quality and are very easy to operate, and need only a radio control system to be installed, fuel to be added and you're virtually off! The main problem with this class is that, as yet, there is no organised racing, as the numbers of these cars are still limited. But don't let this put you off. The cars are great fun and are an excellent way into the 1:8th scale Rallycross class.

ECONOMY 1:8th

The next step up in size is the more traditional 1:8th scale car, powered by a 3.5cc 0.21cu. sized glow engine. The size and scale is the accepted class worldwide in racing events.

The best entry into this level is with one of the less complicated, two-wheel drive cars available from various European manufacturers. These kits are usually 'updatable' at a later stage to full racing specification, and this process can be done gradually spreading the cost over a period of time.

These cars can also come with a recoil starter, which allows for a reduction in initial costs as no starter will be required.

The Kyosho Burns performs well and is easy to build.

The basic Burns kits is an excellent way to start out in Rallycross.

THE COMPETITIVE EDGE

The top end of Rallycross cars is the fully-sophisticated, four-wheel drive Rallycross car used in racing the world over. These cars are produced widely in Europe and in Japan.

The cars are based around a set of rules and regulations for size and configuration and are powered by more highly-tuned 3.5cc engines.

So much for the three main areas. Let's now have a look at the main components in a competition, four-wheel drive Rallycross car — this description will also cover most aspects of the two lower forms of IC racing.

Britain's PB Racing produced these prototype belt drive Rallycross cars.

WHAT MAKES THEM GO

The base for almost all Rallycross cars is a formed aluminium alloy chassis. This is very strong and is usually quite thick (3-4mm). To this, all the components, engine, suspension and radio system are fitted.

For our car to go anywhere, we first need an engine.

As already mentioned, Rallycross cars are powered by 3.5cc engines. Most kits have parts included to fit your engine into the car. This subject is covered in more detail later, as it is an area where the majority of problems are found. The engine is bolted to a set of mounts, which are in turn fixed to the chassis. The engine consists of single cylinder with outlets for the exhaust, carburettor and crankshaft. The carburettor will require an air filter which you will need to obtain separately. The engine will also need a suitable manifold and exhaust. Some kits are supplied with these, otherwise your local dealer will be able to supply you with a suitable exhaust. It is most important not to run an engine without an exhaust — this can cause damage to the model and will be a nuisance to the public, something that must be avoided.

Also supplied in all kits is a clutch mechanism, which allows the engine to keep running when the car is brought to a halt. The clutches are of the centrifugal type and therefore only 'drive' when the engine is revved-up. These are usually quite reliable but must be assembled correctly.

The French-built Yankee car has been both World and European Champion.

STOP AND GO

Now we have a method of going. We also need to be able to stop, Rallycross cars are capable of reaching real speeds of up to 50 mph and therefore in all kits there is a system for stopping the car. Rallycross cars are usually fitted with some sort of disc brake. These are not as on real cars, fitted separately to all wheels, but are placed somewhere on the main drive train. The brakes use a simple cam system with brake discs and pads and are quite capable of stopping the cars quickly from great speeds.

The drive systems on the cars are used to carry the power from the engine to all four, or just two, of the wheels. The drive of these vehicles always uses gears from the engines to a central point but, from there, there are four main ways in which the drive can be transmitted. Chains, belts, gear and shaft drive systems are all used, and it is worth looking at all these systems individually.

Chains Although nowadays chains are rarely used, it is possible you may come into contact with a car that uses chain drive. The main problem with chains is that they do not like the dirt. This leads to higher wear rate and 'stretching', therefore the chains need to be cleaned and lubricated regularly and adjusted continually. Sprockets usually are reliable, if kept clean. The other main disadvantage is the safety aspect — a chain whizzing round is dangerous and should be treated with great respect.

Belts These, too, are rarely found in Rallycross, although they are very popular in 1:10th electric cars. The belts used are made from a soft rubber and Kevlar mix and are of the toothed type. The belts are light and are very reliable and efficient — the main problem is that they need to run completely 'clean'. Protecting these belts is difficult and therefore they have not become popular.

Gears All Rallycross cars without exception, have some sort of gear found in the drive system. I have already mentioned the gears between the clutch and centre lay shaft. The clutch gear or 'bell' is usually steel and has approximately fourteen teeth, although this is adjustable. The main gear onto which this runs is usually plastic and is around four to five times larger. These can be also made in steel but are rarely seen in kits.

The next place gears are normally used is in a crown wheel and pinion that transfer the power through 90 degrees and towards the wheels via the differential. These gears are usually plastic or powdered metal in the kits and are updatable to hardened steel as optional extras. This seems to be an area where many kits fail, and the replacement of these gears is generally a must if much running of the car is to take place.

Shaft Drives By far the most popular drive system in Rallycross cars is that of shafts. These can be relatively light yet very strong, and do not require to be protected from dirt. Usually after the initial gear drive from clutch to layshaft, ball and pin shafts take the drive to both the front and rear gearboxes. This system is efficient and also reliable, and needs very little cleaning or maintenance.

The Mantua range of cars includes their World Champion, Ghibli.

DIFFERENTIALS

For any Rallycross car to handle properly, differentials must be used. The differential takes out the 'bite' or 'twitchiness' of the car by allowing the inside wheel on the car to move less quickly than the outside one — only necessary when cornering.

Most four-wheel drive cars have at least two differentials —

one at the front and one at the rear. Some even have a third centre differential which allows the front and rear of the car to drive at different rates, allowing the car to be driven easily on very slippery surfaces.

There are three main types of differential. Ball diffs are certainly the most simple and have a low number of parts. These are very reliable but must be kept well adjusted. Bevel and spur gear diffs are both slightly more complicated but are widely used in Rallycross cars. They usually have a plastic or aluminium cone which houses the internal gears and are often works of art!

Kyosho Burns with modified suspension — dampers laid horizontally.

Lexan bodyshell fitted to a French Yankee.

FUEL SYSTEMS

Provisions for a fuel system are always given. Most models have a 'hiptop' tank for quick and easy refilling, and these tanks are 125cc, the recognised size. However, not all kits give a system of fuel filtering and this is most important. In the fuel line, a simple filter may be placed. These are cheap and will prolong the life of your engine considerably.

Rallycross cars tend to need more preparation between races.

RALLYCROSS RADIO SYSTEMS

Unlike 1:10th off-road cars, Rallycross cars require a slightly different and upgraded radio system. Because of their size and weight, as well as the added vibrations, fuel spillage and general dirtiness, slightly more expensive radios need to be purchased and extra care taken when fitting them to the model.

Radios will be covered in more detail later on, but generally you must consider the added expense of more powerful servos and high quality radio equipment when costing the price of your model.

Line-up of cars and drivers from the Rallycross World Championships.

4 RADIO CONTROL SYSTEM

Radio control systems have over the past decade become vastly more technical and sophisticated. I have already mentioned radio usage but have not explained the differences between expensive and inexpensive systems.

Before I go into the details and specifications, a brief understanding of what a radio system does and how it works will help.

There are basically four main components to a radio control system. The transmitter (which is held in the hand) sends commands that you give it with your hands to the receiver (which is placed in the car).

The receiver collects these commands and, with the aid of the power pack, tells the servos to move certain amounts in certain directions. All radio systems are 'proportional' which means that the servos move as much or as little as you move the stick on the transmitter.

With this controlled movement in the car via the servos, you can make steering and throttle movements and control the car.

TRANSMITTER

The most popular form of transmitter is the traditional 'box', which has two sticks on the front face used to control the servos. On the left, the control stick moves from top to bottom — this is the throttle (up for forward, back for reverse or brakes). On the right hand side, the control stick moves from left to right – this is the steering. Below or to the left of these control sticks will be two additional smaller levers. These 'trims' are a setting for a neutral point on the servos, i.e. if the car still steers to the left when the main stick is centred, the trim can be made to neutralise the central setting.

Some transmitters have a different set up. American drivers tend to use a system of a trigger for throttle and a wheel for steering. This system has no real advantages, and it is a question of which type of transmitter makes you feel comfortable.

Top-of-the-range radio from Sanwa, comes with carrying case.

FURTHER FEATURES

Sets of radio control equipment are available with just the features already mentioned, with the addition of a meter to inform of the battery power state and a changeable crystal (frequency on which the radio functions).

These bottom-of-the-range radios are designed to use ordinary, dry cell batteries and are perfectly adequate for $\frac{1}{10}$ off-road cars. The sets are generally well-made and give long life.

The next level of radio equipment features a few useful and worthwhile extras. 'Servo reverse' enables the model to be built easier from the start. If, when the stick on a transmitter is moved to the left, the servo rotates clockwise, this may result in the steering on the model moving the wrong way. With 'servo reverse', a simple switch may be moved on the transmitter enabling the servo to move anti-clockwise with the same movement of the control stick. This removes the need to adjust the position of the servo in the car to overcome the problem. The transmitter can be powered by ordinary dry cell batteries. On some sets, a 'charge plug' socket is fitted. This allows the set to be run on Nickel-Cadmium (Ni-cad) batteries that can be re-charged many times for use. If you intend to run your model often, a set of Ni-cad batteries and a charger can soon work out cheaper than buying dry cell batteries on a regular basis. This is also true of the battery supply for the servos. In electric 1:10th cars, the power is taken from the main drive battery but, in 1:8th Rallycross, a battery is needed in the car for the radio and, again, a Ni-cad battery is recommended.

As well as these basic requirements, more sophisticated radio systems have other additional features.

'Steering rates' enable the driver to adjust from the transmitter how much the servo moves when the control stick is fully moved. This is useful in wet or slippery conditions when less steering is required. A rate knob is featured, along with an on-off switch. When the switch is off, the set works as normal, giving full servo movement for full stick movement. When the switch is on, the servo reacts to how much movement is dialed in on the rate knob — anything from 100% movement to as little as 20%.

'End point adjustment' is also a very useful feature. This is used if a model seems to steer more one way than the other. When the control stick is moved completely to one side, the servo will move completely in that direction. If this then needs to be adjusted, it can be done — and also differently for both left and right or full throttle or full brakes.

Another feature often fitted is the function of being able to adjust the setting of the position to which the throttle control stick returns. 'Off settable' throttle sticks can be helpful, mainly on IC cars when more servo movement is needed for the carburettor than for the brakes.

'Exponential rate' is something that is often incorporated on top range radio sets. This is a setting rarely used and also rarely understood. The exponential system allows the first movement of the stick to be 'softened', i.e. if a violent movement of the stick is made, the first 25% of the movement of the servo will be automatically slowed down. This may sound unnecessary, but it can help take out the snatch or wheelspin on the throttle or in-stability on the straight if used on the steering.

PCM or Pulse Code Modulation is a fairly recent innovation and is becoming popular with the 1:8th scale Rallycross fraternity. PCM is a system that eliminates interference — if your model receives an outside source, the PCM system will shut itself down and return to a neutral setting, thus stopping a runaway model. Most helpful!

With the micro chip boom, transmitters are now starting to feature all sorts of gadgets from electronic timers to solar panels! All these extras are helpful but remember it's your own skill, and only that, that will enable you to drive your model successfully.

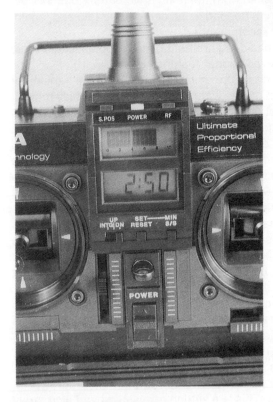

Stop-watches and clocks — the latest features on high tech systems.

SERVOS AND RECEIVERS

As with transmitters, receivers become more sophisticated the more expensive they are. As with most electronic equipment, receivers also tend to be smaller and more compact as you move up through the range. Economy 2 channel (throttle and steering) receivers work very well and nowadays are extremely reliable. Although receivers do come in different price ranges, do not feel you must have an expensive receiver — you should probably spend any of the extra money available on higher quality servos.

What's inside — note the battery pack in the base.

SERVOS

For standard 1:10th cars, economy radio servos are perfectly adequate. The differences between a cheap and expensive servo are the speed at which they move, the strength at which they pull and the amount of weathering protection they have. In 1:10th cars, strength and weather-protection are not too important, due to the low stresses and excellent protection the servos receive. Speed is really the only main area in which a more expensive servo will show any improvement over the 'cheaper' version.

In Rallycross, however, the stresses on the steering of these cars are greatly increased due to their weight. Here, then, is where a stronger and more rugged servo is required. The more expensive servos have stronger electric motors, tougher servo gears and often have rubber 'O' rings sealing out the elements, all of which contribute towards the long life of the servo.

LOOKING AFTER YOUR GEAR

Radio control equipment really needs very little maintenance, so long as you look after it properly. Sometimes your radio gear will get wet, and the best way to 'dry it out' is in an airing cupboard. Remove any batteries or covers and leave it in the cupboard overnight. If your gear does get damp, don't just dump it in the corner — take steps straight away to dry it out and it will probably not suffer.

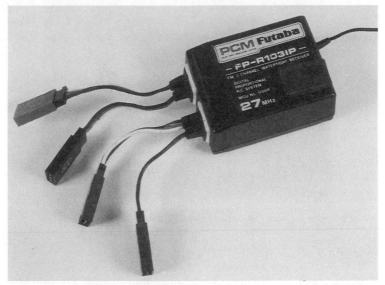

PCM receiver working on 27 MHz.

GENERAL MAINTENANCE TIPS

When you have finished using your transmitter, give it a general clean-up. Fully extend the aerial and clean each section with a dry cloth. Then put a small amount of oil on a rag and run it up and down the aerial, to help it slip in and out of the transmitter. Aerials are generally cheap and, if yours get damaged, it often pays to change it. If you use dry cell batteries, remove them from the case when not using it for long periods of time, as the condition of these batteries can deteriorate. If you have rechargeable Ni-cads in your set, clean the connections regularly as they can coat up. Keep the batteries charged and occasionally cycle them by leaving your transmitter turned on overnight and flattening it. Then recharge straight away — this will prolong the life of the batteries.

The receiver is another article that must be dried out immediately if it gets wet. Take the receiver carefully out of its plastic box and dry in the same way as the transmitter. Check the aerial for any splits or breakages as these all cause interference. Make sure all the plug connections are clean.

Also check over servos regularly. Operate the servos slowly from one side to the next — any odd noises usually mean broken gears and these can be replaced easily. Aerosol cleaning fluid (ozone friendly) is excellent for clean, servo plug leads. Spray the leads regularly to remove any dirt — most servo failures are caused by faulty plugs or leads.

Another source of radio problems is the battery connections and switch harness in the model. This needs to be cleaned regularly, as mud and condensation can often find their way onto the connection surface. Again, aerosol cleaning fluid should be used here.

The final way to assure reliable service from your R/C gear is to send it to the manufacturers at the end of the season for a full service. This is usually a cheap process that will pay dividends. Always package your gear properly if you send it, and make sure it is properly charged.

Adjustment knobs on Futaba's PCM set.

RADIO INSTALLATION

If you are about to install your radio system into your 1:10th car, then you will probably have no problems. Most 1:10th kits have excellent fitting instructions. If, however, you are fitting a radio to a Rallycross car, then there are some helpful tips that will make the task a little easier — although all these tips will be helpful for the 1:10th builder too.

The main area of difficulty is in the setting up of the linkage between the servo and the throttle, brake connections. All linkages follow the same rules. Firstly, you need to mount the servos into the car. All kits give some provisions, some better than others. Servo tape is often used. Both surfaces need to be cleaned thoroughly and free from all oil and grease. Only high-quality servo tape should be used. Radio systems come with rubber grommets to allow for a resilient mounting, and this is most important as a completely solid mounting will cause failure. If possible, do not alter the length of the servo leads — these are designed to be a certain length and should remain that way. A servo saver should be used on the steering. This is a system that allows the servo to be protected from the knocks that they inevitably will receive in an off-road car.

Sanwa's Exerd is a neat system that includes many features.

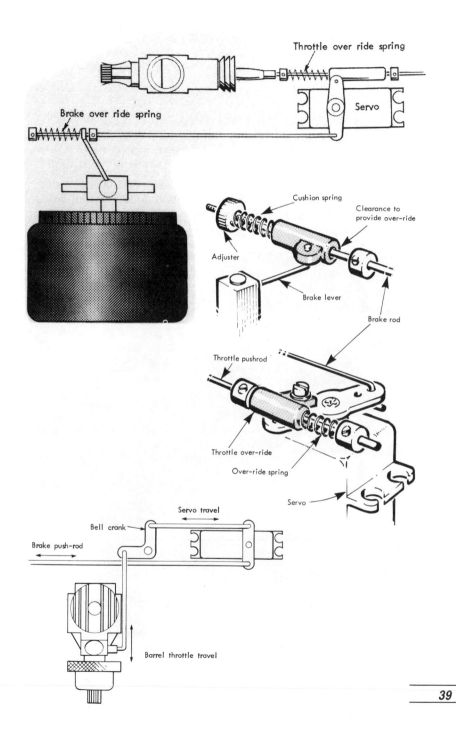

Throttle over ride spring

Brake over ride spring

Servo

Cushion spring

Clearance to provide over-ride

Adjuster

Brake lever

Brake rod

Throttle pushrod

Throttle over-ride

Over-ride spring

Servo

Servo travel

Bell crank

Brake push-rod

Barrel throttle travel

When producing a set of linkages for the throttle/brake movement on a 1:8th car, you must not allow the servo to end up in a 'stall' position. Stalling the servo means that the servo cannot get to the end of its travel — or that it is being stopped from moving. This burns out the motor on the servo and causes irreparable damage. The way to stop this 'stalling' is to use a system of override springs (see diagram on p39). These springs soak up the excess movement and pressures of applying the brakes. All linkages should work at 90 degrees to each other — this stops the servos overriding themselves and prevents them getting stuck in 'stall' positions. Always use high quality joints, preferably of the type which cannot fall off. Make sure all linkages do not bind and that all the movements are free.

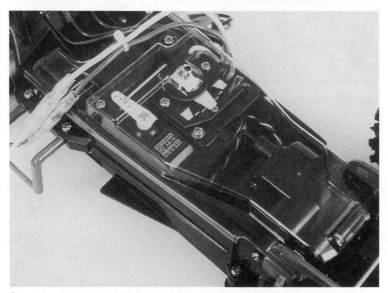

Servo in place connected to a resistor speed controller.

RECEIVER MOUNTING

Receivers are complicated pieces of electronic equipment. They need to be well protected and rubber mounted. High-quality, thick balloons are available from model shops. The receiver should be put into the balloon and the neck sealed with a tie-wrap. This seals out the elements. Receivers should be mounted either on rubber mounts or hung on rubber bands between two posts (see diagram on p41). Bicycle inner tube cuttings are excellent for this and also give added weather protection. Switches also can be protected with a balloon — stretch the balloon over the switch and seal it with a tie-wrap. The switch can still be easily operated.

The various leads from the servos and battery must also be kept neat and tidy. Often, leads wrap themselves around drive shafts causing damage. Keep all the wiring neat by tie-wrapping it down — try not to crimp the wires as this causes splitting of the plastic outer coating.

When using your radio gear, always switch the transmitter on

Standard JR servo with splines on the horn connector.

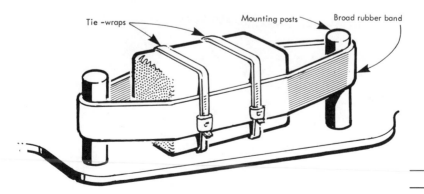

Tie-wraps   Mounting posts   Broad rubber band

first before the car. Also, turn the car off before switching off the transmitters. This will help prolong the life of your radio.

THE RULES

Radio control systems are important pieces of equipment. They should only be used on the legal, government-approved frequencies, for which a list is given. The only two systems allowed in the UK are 27 MHz and 40 MHz. Always make sure that there is no-one in the area where you are using your model, on the same frequency as yourself. It is your responsibility to make sure, for the safety of yourself and others.

5 POWER HOUSE

In all off-road cars, the power to move the vehicle has to come from somewhere. In 1:10th electric cars, this comes from a Ni-cad battery pack, usually of 7.2 volts, powers either a '380' or '540' sized, simple electric motor. The 380 sized motor is only used in 'economy' starter kits. The motors are usually sealed and therefore cannot be cleaned or maintained. The only real tip for longevity is to keep dirt away from the internals and to oil regularly both bushes at either end of the motor.

Kyosho electric 540 motor.

The most widely produced and supplied motor in kits is the mabuchi 540. This simply-engineered motor uses two contact brushes which, as with the 380, is inaccessible, due to the motor being sealed. These mabuchi motors have their brush gear sealed inside the casing (the can). This means they are unserviceable, but their relatively cheap price means that replacement is not an expensive process.

The next in line are 'standard' class motors. These motors have the 'armature' sealed inside the can, but have their brush gear (that requires most maintenance) outside the can, free for maintenance. These motors have metal bearings (brass or white metal) on which the armature runs. They are competitively priced and, with the added advantage of brush replacement, make a good buy.

'Semi' modified motors is the only way to describe the next stage in motor availability. These motors have ball races supporting the armature. This means, again, that life is greatly extended and performance increased. Also, the whole motor is easily taken to pieces for the task of general cleaning and maintenance. This, of course, means that the motors, or at least parts of the motor, have almost indefinite life spans.

Parma 540 motor fitted to a Tamiya Avante.

MODIFIED MOTORS

By far the most powerful of 540 sized motors is the 'modified' range. These motors are based around the can. The cans contain different types of magnet, either standard or wet. These give different performance characteristics — from low revs and high torque to high revs and low torque. The armatures also vary in the amounts of winds and the way the wire is wound onto the armature. For example, a motor which has a single piece of wire wound around the armature twenty times is a '20 single'. A motor which has three pieces of wire wound around the armature seventeen times is a '17 triple'. These different configuarations or 'winds' given different performance, as do the magnets.

Modified motors initially cost more than any others. However, with the ability to maintain these motors by easily replacing brushes and any other defective parts, often this is, in the long term, the cheapest route. The maintenance and care of motors will be covered in a later chapter.

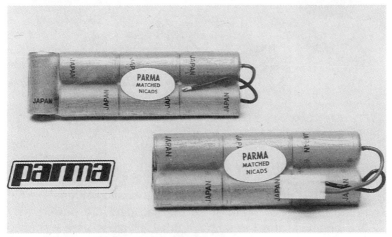

Six and seven cell racing packs from Parma.

NICKEL-CADMIUM BATTERIES

There are various configurations of Ni-cad batteries used in 1:10 electric cars today. Within these configurations, there are three main types of Ni-cad cell. Sanyo produce by far the most cells used in car racing. The three main types are SC, SCR and SCE. Until recently, all these cells have been 1.2 volts and 1.2 mAh. This means the cell's 'pressure' is 1.2 volts and this is universal in all cells used in cars. Where the differences occur are in the mAh rating. SC and SCR cells have a rating of 1.2 mAh. This means their capacity, or 'storage' ability, allows them to deliver their energy at a rate of 1.2 mAh or 1.2 milliamperes per hour. Recently-introduced SCE cells have a higher capacity, i.e. 1.7 mAh. These cells are still the same physical size but give power for a longer period of time, the only disadvantage being the increased expense.

All the internals of a Serpent 3.5cc IC engine.

INTERNAL COMBUSTION ENGINES

There are two main types of internal combustion engine used in off-road cars. The 1:10th scale off-road cars are powered by 2.0cc engines, and the larger 1:8th Rallycross cars by 3.5cc engines. In the 1:10th scale, the engine comes as a complete package with the kit. The engines normally have a recoil starter system already built in. This contains a one-way roller, starting cord and a large return spring. These recoil systems work well and remove the need for an expensive external starter.

Also, the engines are usually supplied with all the other accessories required for running. The exhaust is normally already built onto the engine. This removes the need for finding suitable silencers. Also, air filters and clutch mechanisms are usually pre-fitted, making life extremely easy. These engines are generally well-engineered but, due to their high performance, tend to have a limited life span.

Serpent tuned exhaust pipe/silencer.

3.5cc IC ENGINES

These engines are by far the most popular and are available from a wide range of manufacturers. The engines follow the same basic principles but do have varying specifications. All the engines have a single crankshaft connecting rod and single cylinder/piston. The crankshaft is supported on two ballraces, where the conrod runs, generally on brass bushes. The pistons are made from aluminium, and cylinders are usually brass covered in a very fine layer of hard chrome. The engines mainly have a separate head 'button', this fits into the cylinder and holds the glowplug, then the heatsink bolts onto the crankcase holding the button in place. Some engines have the heatsink and head in one.

There are two configurations of carburettor available. Barrel carburettors have a rotating centre section which opens and closes the carburettor. This system is adopted from aircraft engines used in the past. The more popular and straightforward system is the 'slide' carburettor. These have a simple sliding barrel which moves in and out of the carburettor housing. This allows for simple throttle linkage and enables the carburettor to be opened and shut quickly.

The next main difference between engines — and one that must be considered when purchasing an engine for a car —is the exhaust position. The exhaust can leave the crankcase in two main positions. Side exhaust (S.E.) means just that — the exhaust outlet leaves to one side of the engine. On rear exhaust (R.E.) engines, the exhaust port and outlet faces the rear. The position of the exhaust is important as, in some models, only one of the two types of layout will fit. For this type of engine, you will need to purchase a suitable manifold and exhaust silencer.

Complete 3.5cc engine with carburettor and cooling finned head.

Manifolds are generally manufacturered by the kit makers to suit their own car, although engine manufacturers also produce ranges of manifolds.

Basically, the manifold should follow as smooth a line as possible (no sharp bends) to allow the exhaust gases to flow out easily. The manifolds are either rubber mounted with springs or are directly bolted to the crankcase. Next are the exhausts. These are available in various shapes and sizes, but remember, as with manifolds, choose one that suits your vehicle, but most

importantly is BRCA, EFRA or FEMCA approved. This guaran-
tees the silencer is just that, and keeps your engine quiet!

There are many types of glowplug available for use in your
engine. Some engines are supplied with plugs. They will not last
forever, so always carry some spares. There are various 'hot'
and 'cold' plugs available but generally a 'mid' range plug is
most suitable.

6 RACE PREPARED

There are, of course, many similarities between the building of 1:10th and 1:8th cars. General good building tips cover both, but there are areas in which the different scales require special attention — and these will be pointed out where necessary. The set up of the suspension and damping is a separate subject that will be covered later. What will be covered now are general hints and tips for building your car.

Completed Schumacher Procat, minus bodyshell.

TOOL UP

It is most important that you have the right tools. Most kits include some of the tools required, i.e. allen keys and a small box spanner. What is required is a selection of hand tools that are suitable for the kit you are about to build. You will need pliers, cutters and spanners, as well as correctly-fitting screwdrivers. Take screws from the kit and, if necessary, buy a good quality driver that fits correctly. Also thread-locks, paint and a modelling knife will almost certainly be the minimum requirements to finish off your model.

Neat, light toolbox, ideal for tools and spares.

A PLACE TO START

It really is no good assembling a kit on the living room floor. What you need is a good solid workbench, one which is not important if it gets damaged. Also, good lighting is essential, as well as good ventilation (if soldering and painting is to take place). Once you have your workbench, a selection of paint tops or any small plastic containers are useful for keeping parts in.

WHERE TO START

There is only one place to start and this is with the manufacturer's instructions. Even before opening the box, read these through at least once — even if this is not your first kit. Once you have read these, look at the parts and where they are. Familiarise yourself with the parts as this will save time later.

Most kits have their parts in sealed bags. Keep the screws, etc, together in the plastic containers, as the instructions will refer to the parts as a group. DON'T MIX THEM UP!

The motor fitted in place. Keep all wiring neat.

Set the gears with a small amount of play.

WILL IT STAY TOGETHER?

Most 1:10th car kits have excellent instructions. Even for the complete beginner, so long as the instructions are adhered to, a successful model is virtually guaranteed. Where most problems occur is that, after initial running, parts of the model start to come loose or fall off — this is even more the case with 1:8th cars. It is impossible to explain how tight a screw should be tightened — in plastic, self tappers should not be given extreme pressure. As soon as the two parts come together just a simple 'nip' will ensure tightness without stripping the plastic. In some cases, some form of loctite will be required. This comes in varying strengths from 'soft' to 'permanent'. For model car use generally, a 'mild' loctite is sufficient for those parts which have a tendency to fall apart. Only after experience and practice will you learn 'how tight' or whether loctite is required. So, if something tends to come loose, use a soft loctite.

Ready-to-run cars often include instructions in case of need for repair.

BASIC CONSTRUCTION

Make sure that you follow the order of construction shown in the instructions. Time will be wasted if, due to not following the instructions, parts need to be taken to pieces to allow for stages in building. Always clean-up all the parts before assembly. All plastic parts should be carefully examined and any sprue or moulding marks should be removed with a modelling knife. All metal parts should also be cleaned up and any burrs removed.

The chassis forms the main base to which all the components will be fixed. This needs to be square and flat. When assembling the chassis, keep it on the workbench, gradually tightening all screws in a criss-cross pattern from front to rear. This will allow the chassis to remain unstressed and square.

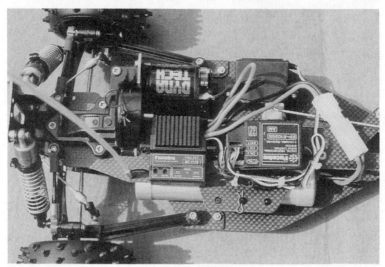

Radio installed — try to keep the wiring tucked out of harm's way.

SUSPENSION

For the suspension to work correctly, it must be free, with no notchiness or tight spots. A guide to deciding whether the suspension is free enough is to remove all dampers and roll bars. If the car is turned upside down, all the suspension arms should fall easily — not sticking, i.e. they should be free under their own weight. If this is not the case, there are a number of reasons why.

Most suspension arms either pivot on a steel pin or on some form of ball joint. The plastic arms should be cleaned up so that all pins move freely. This can be done with the correctly-sized reamer — drills or files should be avoided as they tend to produce an 'oval' hole which will soon wear out. Ball joints can sometimes be cleaned up by placing the ball into a drill. Spin the ball and clean it up with fine wet and dry sandpaper — then polish with T-cut, which usually allows for free movement. Drive shafts can often cause stiff suspension. The shafts should have a small amount of free play at all times — this can usually be adjusted with a small grub screw on the driveshaft. Some kits include runner 'O' rings — these are often fitted to the diff drive cup and this can take up any excessive play.

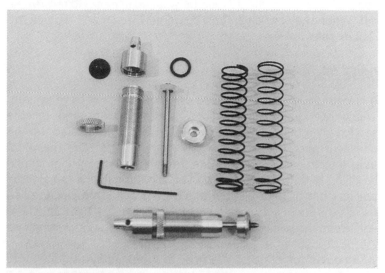

The components which come together to form an oil damper.

BEARINGS

Obviously, different kits have different specifications. Some kits have plastic bearings, some have brass and some have high-quality, sealed ballraces.

The plastic bearings must be kept well lubricated if they are to last. The enemy of these bearings is dirt — although obviously oil and grease tend to attract dirt. The only real guide is to clean the bearings regularly (especially those most prone to the dirt) and re-oil. Brass or white metal bearings have much the same problems, although they tend to last longer. These again should be cleaned and oiled regularly. Keep a close eye on the bearings and replace them as soon as they show too much wear.

Both plastic and brass bearings can be replaced by ballraces. All manufacturers offer 'hot-up' kits and ballraces are certainly the first choice that should be considered when updating your model.

If your kit contains ballraces, or you intend to update them, they still require regular attention — they cannot just be left for long periods of time. Most ballraces have rubber seals. Dirt, mainly dust, manages to get behind these seals, making them stiff and generally rough.

The ballrace shield can be easily removed with a modelling knife. The ballrace should then be washed in petrol to remove all dirt. When they are clean and spin freely, re-oil and replace the rubber shields.

DRIVE BELTS

A large number of $\frac{1}{10}$ cars use drive belts in their drive system. These are generally excellent, giving efficient and reliable service. The belts, however, can, if incorrectly adjusted, be the cause of poor handling and low running time. The manufacturer's instructions clearly state the amount of play that should be given to these belts — however, a good guide is to have the belt as loose as possible, but with no slippage. This slippage can usually be identified as a 'clicking' noise under hard acceleration. Keep the belts clean and do not crimp the belts — these are the usual causes of failure.

Various sizes of gears are used in the drive system of 1:10th cars. The three types mainly used are the 32dp, 48dp and 0.6 module, and they refer to the size and number of teeth on the gears. The mesh of these gears is most important. Normally, the smallest of the gears is made from aluminium or steel, the largest from plastic. The setting of these gears should allow for a small amount of play.

3.5cc carburettor — has a ridge to which the filter should be fitted.

ELECTRIC BITS

A lot of problems can arise with the radio installation. Kits for 1:10th cars lay out the installation clearly but things can still go wrong. If, after fitting the servos into the car and adjusting the trims on the transmitter, the car still steers to one side when it should be going straight, the servo horn or servosaver should be removed and adjusted on the splines. If the speed controller causes problems, i.e. sticking in forward, then this is often the same problem. Turn your radio on — set the trim to the centre and adjust the servo horn to line up in the 'off' position of the controller. Often, making adjustments on the trim will cure any problems after the servo horns are in the correct place.

Receivers and battery packs should be properly and securely placed on the chassis. If the kit supplies servo tape, you must make sure that both surfaces are perfectly clean. Use either lighter fuel or motor spraycleaner, and rub the two surfaces with a clean tissue. Do not touch the receiver or surface with your hands, as this will not allow the tape to stick.

Above all, good building and reliability is mainly about thoroughness and tidiness. Keep your wiring neat, and tie-wrap any excess leads out of harm's way. Try to place your receiver away from the electric motor — otherwise, you may get interference.

All gears should run smoothly with no notchiness.

PRIDE AND JOY

Your model will be finished off with the combination of the bodyshell and wings. In the low range 1:10th car kits, hard plastic bodyshells are included. These can be easily painted with an enamel paint and, when dry, the stickers applied. These shells require little, if any, cutting out, and they look very smart with very little effort. The main problem is that these bodies are brittle and need to be carefully looked after if they are to remain in one piece.

Lexan is a tough clear plastic which is widely used in off-road bodyshells. Large sheets of 1mm thickness lexan are vacuum formed over moulds to produce bodyshells, undertray and wings. The main advantage of this material is that it is incredibly strong and light. The main disadvantage is that it can be difficult to cut out accurately and is rather more difficult to paint than its hard plastic brother. The main problem with the painting is that lexan bodyshells are painted on the inside, which can be tricky.

Cutting out the lexan bodyshell can appear to be quite difficult. With a chinagraph pencil, draw around the areas that need to be removed. Then carefully and slowly run a modelling knife over the mark, scoring into the lexan. This does not need to be deep — it just needs to score the surface. Once the surface has been scored, it is only a matter of bending the lexan back and forth until it breaks. A clean break is usually achieved — this then only requires a light rub over with sandpaper to remove the sharp edge. If you do not feel confident, practise on the spare material that you will later discard from around the bodyshell. Any tricky areas can be easily cut away using a sharp pair of scissors, although caution must be taken while cutting out any bodyshell. Knives and scissors can be dangerous. Once you have cut out the shell (remember to do all cutting while the shell is clear), then wash it thoroughly in warm soapy water — this prepares the shell for masking and painting.

PAINT YOUR WAGON

The masking and preparation time is when the look of your bodyshell will be decided. Even in today's weird and wonderful car body shapes, windows need to be left clear and any stripes or patterns need to be masked up. Once the bodyshell is washed, make sure that it is completely dry. Draw with chinagraph pencil on the outside of the shell where you would like the windows to be. Also any stripes or different coloured areas should also be sketched on. You can use frisk film, or even sticky back contact, to mask the shell. Place the masking film inside the shell and stick it over the area, then carefully trace onto the film the outline of the windows with a pencil. Remove the film, stick it onto a clean piece of glass and cut it out using a sharp knife. Then replace the film onto the bodyshell lining up with the window — make sure all the edges are properly pushed down so that the paint cannot bleed under the film. At this stage, you must also decide on any section of the bodyshell you would like in different colours — mask these using the same methods as for the windows.

When spraying lexan it is best to spray your dark colours first, then gradually work towards the lighter colours, i.e if you want your car black, blue and white, spray the colours in that order from dark to light, otherwise when black is sprayed behind white, the white on the bodyshell will appear 'dirty'.

Ready for the off! Body painted ready for the race track!

Special lexan paints are available in either spray can form or in tins for use with airbrushes. The spray cans give a good result, although airbrushes do tend to give a more accurate finish. Spray three or four thin coats of paint, rather than one thick coat to cover the surface. Lexan paint tends to dry quickly and only five to ten minutes between coats is necessary. Be careful when unmasking your bodyshell as, although the paint may appear fully dry, it is likely still to be soft and prone to scratching for at least 24 hours. Finish your bodyshell off with stickers and race numbers — try not to fit on too many stickers, as this can look overcrowded and messy.

Once the bodyshell is finished, it is possible to sustain the life of the shell by some simple tricks. Where the bodyshell fits to the chassis, e.g. overbody posts, strengthen the shell with some thick carpet tape. This stops the shell ripping during accidents. Also, if any rips or tears start in the shell, don't just leave them — try to round them off and strengthen them again with tape.

7 CHARGE-UP

All radio controlled 1:10th cars use Ni-cad rechargeable batteries. These batteries are the sole source of energy for the main drive motor, and often the radio control system. Nickel Cadmium 'sub C' sized cells are the accepted radio control car form of energy. These cells are 1.2 volt and are either 1.2 or 1.7 Ah. The major characteristic of these batteries is their ability to deliver very high current (60/80 amps [A]) for short periods of time.

Most 1:10th cars use six of these sub 'C' cells and this gives a pack voltage of 7.2 volts (6 x 1.2v). This determines how fast the motor will be able to turn. The ampere-hour rating gives the storage ability, in radio control cars either 1.2 or 1.7 A for one hour.

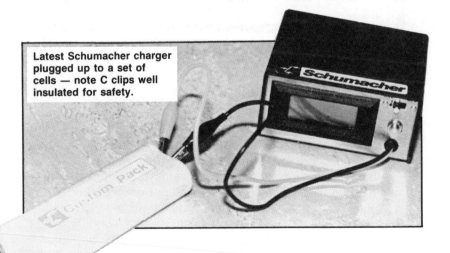

Latest Schumacher charger plugged up to a set of cells — note C clips well insulated for safety.

While charging the Ni-cads, towards the end of the charge the cell will produce heat and this builds up rapidly as part of a chemical reaction, which results in the chemical turning to gas and evacuating the cell. Therefore, you must stop charging before this reaction takes place. There are various ways of doing this.

First, let's look at how cells charge. Then, let's consider the various systems available for getting the most from your Ni-cads.

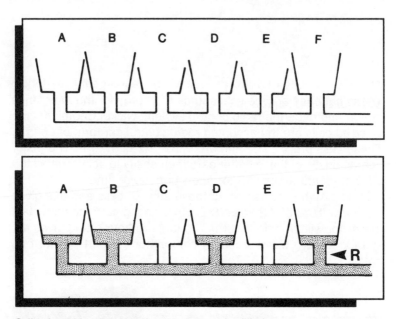

Cells should be thought of as buckets to be filled.

HOW THEY CHARGE

To understand how a pack of cells accepts a charge, you should think of the six cells in the pack as six buckets of waters (see above diagram), each connected to a hose. When charged, water is pushed into the buckets at a certain rate (R).

Although the capacity of each bucket is 1.2 Ah this is only in name, not reality. In practice, each cell or bucket of the six has a slightly different capacity. When water is pushed in at (R), the smaller buckets 'C' and 'E' will fill up first, and the largest bucket 'B' will fill last. This is the equivalent of the smaller buckets 'C' and 'E' being over-filled or over-charged and getting hot. When all the buckets are full (or all cells hot), this is fully charged.

During use, water or power is drawn at the same rate from all the buckets. This means that the small capacity buckets will empty first, then the pack of cells or group of batteries is only giving power (or water) from four of the six, eventually only bucket 'B' (the largest) is giving power (or water). This would be a one cell pack, which is useless.

This can best be seen in radio controlled cars when the car appears to go 'slow', not necessarily flat but going at a slower rate. This happens when two or three of the cells are empty. What is important to note is that it is better by far to have all your batteries (or buckets) with the same capacity — this will give a longer period of useful energy.

CHOOSING BATTERIES

What would be perfect is a pack of batteries that has limitless capacity and lasts for ever! This, I'm afraid, is impossible. As explained, it is best to have a pack of cells in which all six cells have a similar capacity — these packs are available and are generally known as 'matched' cell. What must be decided is whether the extra cost of a set of 'matched' cells is worth the extra running time.

Standard battery packs are available with a capacity of 1.2 Ah — these are also available as matched packs which are, of course, better. Also, packs are available of 1.7 Ah, again in standard and 'matched' packs.

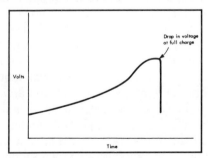

Typical peak voltage curve.

BATTERY CHARGING AND CARE

Almost all battery packs come already assembled and fitted with one of a number of leads. If the lead you require is fitted, fine!

If not, always solder battery connections, and do not crimp, twist or tape wires together — this can cause accidents. Always use a male/female plug so that connections can only be made one way round.

There are only four main ways in which to charge Ni-cad batteries, but they all have one thing in common — the initial power source. This is normally a 12 volt car battery. This will have to be in a full state of charge before any further Ni-cad charging can occur. If you have a 12 volt battery, always store it safely and, if you transport it, put it in a plastic bucket — this avoids it falling over and prevents spillages. It is possible to charge straight from a car but, be warned, don't let your car battery get too flat and don't charge from the car while it's running.

Batteries must not be charged or connected straight to a 12 volt battery or from a mains socket — these are both very dangerous.

The first method of charging is the manual set up. Some kits come supplied with a charge lead. This lead is either made from resistance wire or has a resistor in the circuit. This is a simple process to charge. The black lead, or negative (-ve), connects from the negative of the 12 volt to the (-ve) of the battery pack. The positive lead (+ve) connects from the (+ve) side of the 12 volt to the (+ve) of the battery pack. Once this is underway, the charge will take around 20-30 minutes. When the battery becomes slightly warm to the touch, it is charged — the battery should never be allowed to get hot. The main disadvantage to this system is that of 'overcharging', if for any reason the battery is left unattended. If overcharging does occur — i.e. the battery gets very hot or spits or pops — remove it from charge and put it onto a hard surface. Do this with a stick — do not touch the pack as it will be red hot! Cover the pack with a bucket or similar and leave it alone. The pack will take around an hour to cool off, and you will probably have to throw it away and start again.

The second method of charging is with a timer. This is usually in the form of a resistor matched up to a clockwork timer. All that needs to be done is for the charger to be correctly connected up to the 12 volt and the battery pack. Set the timer for 15 minutes — if the battery is still cool, give the charger another 10 minutes. When the pack is just warm, the battery is charged. These chargers are simple and safe as, if you forget about the pack, the timer automatically shuts off the charge.

The third method of charging is that of 'peak detection'. These chargers again connect to a 12 volt battery and to the pack. During charging, the voltage in the pack rises until the pack is fully charged. This voltage is much higher than the rated 7.2 volts — even as high as 10 volts. At this point the pack becomes warm and the voltage starts to drop. The 'peak detection' unit inside the charger senses this drop and turns off the charger. Again, this is a safe method which stops the danger of over-charging.

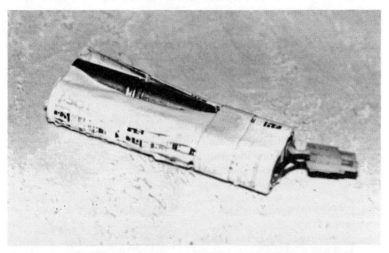

An overcharged battery — note the heat shrink has melted and split.

The fourth and most popular method of charging in racing circles is that of 'temperature sensing'. This again uses the same system of being connected to a 12 volt battery and to the battery pack. The cut-off point is decided by a small sensor which is placed on the cells. When the temperature is reached, that means the cells are charged and the charge is automatically turned off.

Generally, to get the most from your cells, temperature sensing charging works best. Peak detection chargers are generally safer but are expensive, although they usually pay dividends with longer cell life and consistent charging. Most experienced car drivers use temperature sensing chargers although, if you feel unsure about this method, don't be tempted — go for a peak detection unit.

GENERAL CHARGING HINTS

Try to charge your cells so that you use them straight after you finish charging them. If this is not possible, charge early and reheat or peak the cells (this won't take long) just before you use them. This gives maximum results.

After use, your Ni-cad will be very hot, almost too hot to hold in the hand. This is generally acceptable although, if the cells are really too hot to touch, this is a sign of overgearing or a restriction in the car's drive train.

Once your cells have cooled off, after use connect them to a discharge resistor of some type. This can be a 60 watt car bulb or a 1 ohm resistor. When the pack is completely flat (the bulb out, the resistor cold), store the batteries away for their next use.

Ni-cads seem to develop a 'memory' when always discharged to a certain voltage. After a period, the Ni-cads will not perform below this method. Fully discharging the Ni-cads avoids this and sustains their effectiveness.

Before recharging Ni-cad packs, they must be completely cool. Do not continue to recharge a warm pack — this will drastically reduce the life and voltage of the pack.

Parma produce specialised packs of cells to suit various installations.

SOLDERING CELLS

Sometimes leads can come off and battery packs can come apart — this then necessitates soldering. Try to solder cells after they have just been discharged — this is when they are still warm. Clean the cell with emery cloth and twist any wire so that it stays together. Use a powerful 40 watt soldering iron. The trick is to heat the cell for the minimum time — this stops damage to the cell. Always 'tin' the wire first, and only hold the iron on to the cell for a couple of seconds. Don't forget to use a high quality solder.

FINAL POINTS

Only buy your Ni-cads from reputable high volume outlets. Do not buy the cheapest or most expensive Ni-cads available. When soldering connectors to leads, be careful of the polarity and always use foolproof connectors. Invest in either a 'peak detection' or 'temperature sensing' charger and a good quality 12 volt car battery. Discharge cells after use and do not ever charge a hot battery.

Lastly, a warning — Ni-cads can be dangerous when hot. If overcharging occurs, leave them alone to cool down.

Do not ever connect a charge pack together — this could result in an explosion. Follow these simple rules and your batteries will last you for 200-300 charges. Lastly, do not dispose of Ni-cads in incinerators or in an open fire.

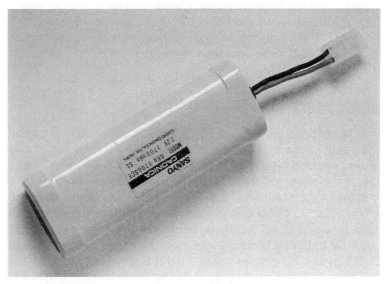

The latest innovation — 1700 mAh racing cells.

8 CLEAN UP

Getting the most from your electric motor is a matter of good care, preparation and correct selection of gear ratio. For a motor to work well, it must be installed properly, be securely connected electrically to the speed controller, and have a clean commutator with a good brush contact. These are the very basics for all electric motors and these rules must be followed by everybody.

There are two main designs in motors. The 'mabuchi' has a fully enclosed brush gear and allows no access to any of the internals. The more popular type is the 'Yokomo', which has an exposed brush gear and can be easily taken to pieces for maintenance.

MOTOR PARTS

The largest part of the motor is the metal part which is held in the hand — this is called the can. The can is blanked off at one end to enclose a bearing from which a shaft protrudes. This is the main shaft to which the iron core copper windings and commutator are joined. This shaft runs the whole length of the motor. The 10-15mm of the shaft which protrudes is where the gear pinion is fixed. At the other end of the motor is a plastic moulded end, which carries two metal plates. These are secured to the plastic by a small screw, and a large rivet.

These plates are each side of the centre line of the motor and are bent to form a channel. They hold the motor brushes and are called the brush holders. The small screw also holds a small tug which is joined, via a copper braid, to the motor brush. The brush is held in the channel on the brush holder by a small spring. This spring sits on the spring post and holds the brush up against the commutator. Also in this plastic moulded end is another bearing which holds the other end of the shaft.

Whether your kit came with a motor or you have bought a new motor, the same procedures of running in and care apply. Do not rush out to buy a new 'faster' motor straight away. Use the motor in your kit — it will certainly be adequate if you are learning to drive.

All mechanical objects require some sort of running in. The object of running in an electric motor is to bed the brushes in to the shape of the com. When new, the gaps between the brushes and com cause electricity to jump across, causing sparks. This generates heat and wears away the com and brushes — not desirable.

Reedy 540 motor with cooling brush holders.

There are two ways to run your motor in properly. The easiest, although not the best, is to put the motor into the car and to drive it gently on a hard surface. Do not use reverse or brake, and only accelerate very gently, reaching full speed slowly.

The best way to go about this is to follow these basic rules. Take your new motor and examine it, making sure that everything is in order. Solder the connections on correctly, red to +ve and black to -ve, fit a pinion onto the motor and, before installing, lubricate each bearing with a small drop of 3 in 1 oil. Don't forget to solder on two suppressors, unless your motor already has these fitted. Correctly align the gear on the motor into the car. With a fully charged Ni-cad, slowly run the car on tarmac. Accelerate very gently and allow the car to roll freely often. As you come towards the end of the first five minutes, gradually accelerate faster until you use full power quickly. Do not use reverse or brakes. Do this three times before cleaning (explained later).

By far the best way to run in a motor, however, takes a little more effort and time. Take your new motor and connect the necessary connections and suppressors. Now you need a charged four cell pack. After placing a small amount of oil on each bearing, allow the motor to run on the four cell pack for 20 minutes. After this, allow the motor to cool. Take out the brushes and clean them using a cotton bud and spray motor cleaner. Using another cotton bud (soaked in cleaner), push it down the brush holder and rotate the motor, cleaning the com. Reassemble the motor and run for a further 5 minutes. This motor will now require a clean before proper use.

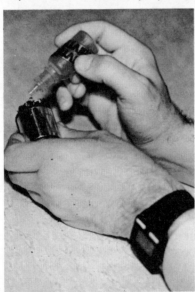

Dripping motor cleaner onto the com.

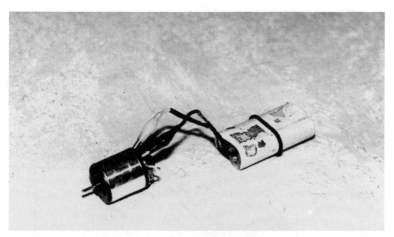

The motor connected to a 4 cell pack being run in.

MOTOR CARE AND CLEANING

To look after your motor properly, you should remove it after every race. Firstly, check that there is no notchiness in the bearings and that it runs freely. You will need a box of cotton buds and a tin of motor spray. After every race, clean the face of the brushes and the commutator. This removes any dirt or oil build-up and prolongs brush life while keeping good performance. Release the brush spring and swing it round clear of the brush holder. Take the spring off the post and pull out the brush. Take a cotton bud, and spray motor cleaner onto it until it is soaked. Push the cotton bud down the brush holder until it touches the com, rotate the motor several times and remove the cotton bud. The end of the cotton bud will be black. Now wipe the clean edge of the bud across the face of the brush. Repeat this for the other side of the motor — you may need to clean the com 3-4 times before it is properly clean. Now replace the brushes and springs and the motor is ready for running.

After every 10-15 runs, the motor will require a more thorough clean. Take the motor out of the car, place it on a rag on the bench and run the motor by connecting it to the battery. Spray motor spray down the brush holders while the motor is running — do this twice down each brush holder. Now repeat the cotton bud cleaning process and your motor will be ready to run.

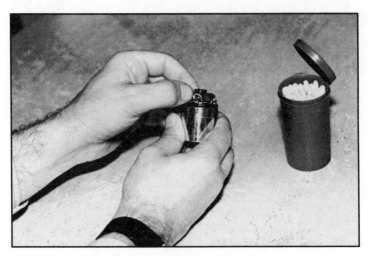

Unhook springs then carefully remove brush.

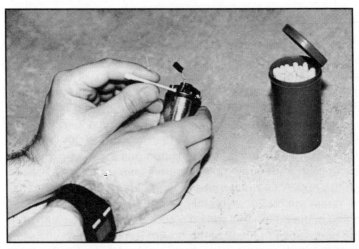

Soak cotton bud in spray and clean down brush holder until it reaches the com.

MAJOR CLEAN-UP

After 10 to 20 runs, or if you run your car in water or mud, your motor may need a proper dismantle and clean.

Firstly, place a clean piece of rag on the bench on which to place all the parts — remember where the washers and screws

Apply light pressure on the cotton bud and rotate armature.

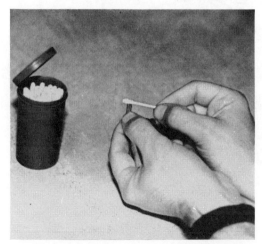

Remove brush and clean with cotton bud twice.

go. Remove the brushes and springs as before. With a marker pen, draw a small mark onto the can and onto the end bell (plastic cap which holds brushes). Undo the two small screws which hold the brush taps to the end bell — normally a washer will be stuck to the bearing on the end bell, so remove this with a pair of tweezers. Now pull the armature from the can. Again, washers may be on the arm or stuck inside the can, so remember how many washers go at each end of the arm.

Clean the can with a piece of rag. You may need to wash it out with motor spray — again, finish it off by cleaning it with a rag wrapped around your finger. Clean the end bell with a dry brush to remove any dust. The bearing may need a spray with cleaner to remove dirt. Clean and replace the washers onto the com, and carefully replace the com into the can making sure the washers do not fall off. Now replace the end bell — lining up the mark you made earlier. Replace the screws and tighten them up. Go through the cotton bud cleaning process and refit the springs and brushes. Oil the bearings, and your motor is ready for use.

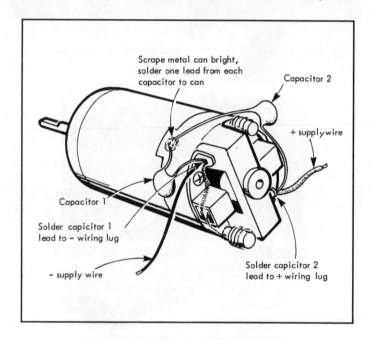

Scrape metal can bright, solder one lead from each capacitor to can

Capacitor 2

+ supply wire

Capacitor 1

Solder capicitor 1 lead to – wiring lug

– supply wire

Solder capicitor 2 lead to + wiring lug

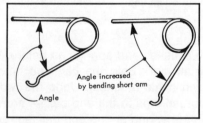

Angle increased by bending short arm

Angle

Motor capacitor fitting and brush springs.

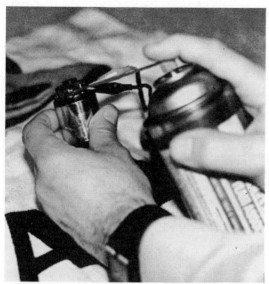

Spray motor cleaner down the brush holder, while turning armature — it's not easy!

MOTOR ADDITIVES

Generally, motor additives are used mainly by the real racers — they can improve performance if used correctly but, if used incorrectly, can cause damage to motors. Various types of sprays and liquids are available and, in general, should be avoided. The additives attempt to get between the brushes and com and soften them both, allowing for better contact. This causes faster wear and large build-ups of dirt. If you use motor additives, follow the instructions and clean your motor thoroughly between runs.

SPRINGS AND BRUSHES

The most important aspect of brush springs is that they apply equal pressure onto each brush. This can be checked by looking at the springs together, making sure that they are bent at the same angle between the long and short arm. Basically, the larger the angle, the harder the spring pushes on the brushes. Some springs have an angle of 70° some up to 180°, and a good average point is around 110°. Keep a careful eye on the springs and don't bend them too often — otherwise they will break.

Basically, brushes are consumable items. Once they have

worn down, they should be changed, so check your brushes regularly for any signs of wear, especially deep scoring. If this is seen, change the brushes immediately as dirt has imbedded itself into the brush.

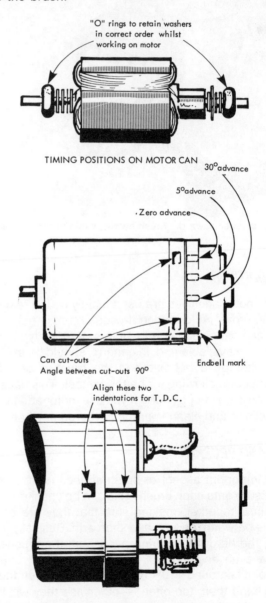

"O" rings to retain washers in correct order whilst working on motor

TIMING POSITIONS ON MOTOR CAN

30°advance

5°advance

Zero advance

Can cut-outs
Angle between cut-outs 90°

Endbell mark

Align these two indentations for T.D.C.

Armature and motor can detail — note zero advance point.

Always change brushes in pairs and try to use only reputable manufacturers' products. Remember that the brushes carry all the current to the motor and should be looked after.

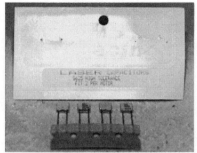

Capacitors which need to be placed on all motors.

The equipment required to keep a motor in good running condition.

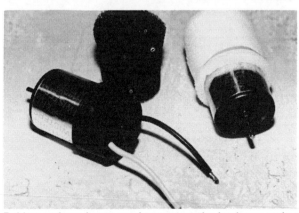

Rubber or foam boots used to protect the business ends of motors.

CONCLUSIONS

Ultimate speed is not the 'be all and end all' in radio controlled cars. Choose your motors carefully — it is much better to have one modified motor than a handful of standard motors. Keep a good supply of cotton buds and quality motor spray. Do not be tempted to run the motor continually without cleaning.

Lastly here is a simple list of *DOs* and *DON'Ts* for motor care.
DO run in all new motors carefully, either in a car or on the bench.
DO clean the brushes and com after every run with a cotton bud soaked in motor spray.
DO clean the motor regularly by spraying with cleaner while the motor is running on the bench.
DO fit capacitors to all motors (at least two).
DO select the correct ratio and make sure the motor gear is correctly lined up.
DO regularly change motor brushes
DO oil the bearings after each clean-up.
DON'T use a new motor in a car at full speed straight away.
DON'T put a modified motor in a kit without changing ratio (refer to motor packaging).
DON'T run a car with stiff gearboxes or a stiff drive train.
DON'T run brushes more than $\frac{1}{3}$ worn down.
DON'T continually run a motor without cleaning it — it will not last.
DON'T over-oil bearings — a small drop will always do.
DON'T over-use motor additives — they will eventually ruin your motor unless you take very good care of it.

9 KEEP IN TOUCH

There are two main types of speed controller — mechanical resistor and electronic. The mechanical resistor types are the ones which come in kits.

RESISTOR TYPES

Resistor type speed controllers are operated by a servo. The servo moves the actuating arm via a small wire link. This, in turn, moves the switching system on the controller.

Most speed controllers supplied today have a set of fixed resistors. These are brought into the circuit by means of a wiper board switch. The resistors are mounted separately to the wiper board, usually in a position to aid heat dissipation. The controllers work by the servo moving the arm on the board, which switches on the resistors in turn, allowing more and more current to flow to the motor. During slow speeds, the resistors use up power by giving off heat.

The wiper boards usually have three positions, and the connections are made by a slider arm passing over a printed circuit board. This, of course, can wear out and is a source of lost energy.

These resistor speed controllers are very inefficient, as they simply dump energy as heat. This is not desirable as only a limited amount of energy is available to a 1:10 car, i.e. the battery pack.

These controllers are fine as a starting point, but do require the circuit board to be cleaned regularly and replaced once pitting of the connections occurs. They often also have a connection to power the radio control system, removing the need for a separate battery pack.

Speed controller fitted to the rear shock bracket.

ELECTRONIC SPEED CONTROLLERS

The first major difference you will notice about electronic speed controllers is the price. Even top-of-the-range resistor speed controllers cost very little when compared to electronic ones.

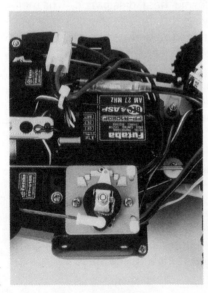

Resistor board controller fitted in the car and connected via a link to the servo.

Electronic speed controllers are infinitely more efficient than the resistor types. It should be stressed, however, that they are in no way indestructible and that any repair cost will far exceed those incurred with resistor types.

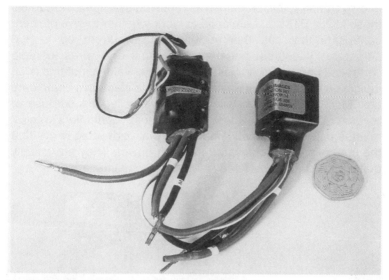

Nowadays electronic controllers can be very small.

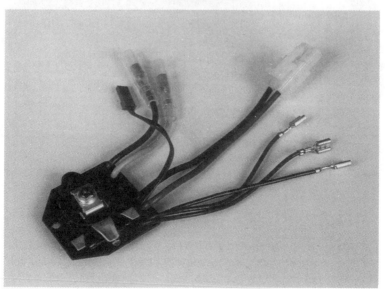

The Tamiya resistor speed controller — tough and cheap.

When electronic speed controllers first made an appearance, the only type of transistors available were the bi-polar type. These were expensive and were not ideal, and actually used up some of the power. With the introduction of high power MOSFET's, which are an inexpensive and efficient form of energy transfer, this problem was removed overnight. Nowadays these MOSFETs can be placed to work together to give efficient controllers that can theoretically handle current up to 300 amperes. Of course, battery connections and wires in radio controlled cars could not take these power values, but this is an indication of how highly developed today's electronic controllers are. Most of these controllers use a relay for the purpose of reverse. This is where most power is lost. Controllers without reverse can be extremely small. The main advantages are that the controllers do not waste too much power. They are usually quite small and, once fitted, require little maintenance.

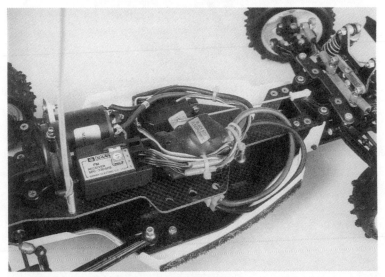

Black Box controller fitted to a Tamiya Egress.

SETTING UP AND USE

All manufacturers provide different types of adjustments for setting up the controllers. If reverse is fitted, the position at which this works is usually adjustable, as is the position for full power and the 'off' position.

Neat KO controller fitted to a Yokomo YZ10 at the World Championships.

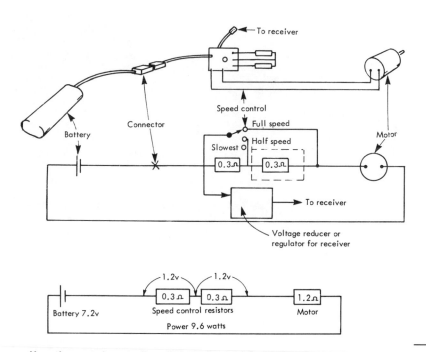

How the speed controllers fit into the model car electric circuit.

Some of the more sophisticated controllers have heat-sensitive devices which shut down the controller when over-heating occurs.

The most important rules for use of any speed controllers are, firstly, that when fitting to the car, check and double check the polarities — all today's controllers are polarity conscious, i.e. they need to be plugged in the right way round or they will blow-up.

Secondly, never put unnecessary forces onto the controller by operating the car while it is in a stalled position, i.e. trying to run the car when the wheels cannot turn.

10 INTERNAL COMBUSTION ENGINES

When buying the engine for your car, there will be a number of choices you will need to make – 3.5cc engines come in varying forms and specifications. Car engines are available made especially to cope with the extra problems incurred in running in Rallycross cars. Before you choose an engine, you must make sure it is compatible with your car.

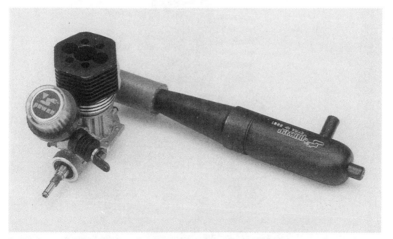

Exhaust and filter fitted — only the clutch remains to be bolted on.

CRANKSHAFT AND EXHAUST

In your kit there will be a clutch and flywheel system. This will fit onto one of two types of crankshaft available. Some engines have a 6mm or ¼ UNF thread on the crankshaft. This is where the flywheel which houses the clutch is bolted. You must inspect your kit to see if this is the one you require, or whether the 'SG' type crankshaft is the one you need. The 'SG' crankshaft has a ground flat section on which the clutch bearings run. These two shafts are very different and the correct choice must be made. Either check the instructions of your kit or refer to your local dealer.

Your next decision is whether your engine is to be side or rear exhaust. The instructions in your kit will advise on this.

The most widely-used and suitable engine is the 'car' range available from most manufacturers. These engines produce most of their power low down in the rev range, the ideal place for cars. They also have large cooling heads to take away the heat. Most of these engines also have slide carburettors with good mountings for air filters. When buying your engine, go for a mid-priced model, and make sure it is ballraced and suits your application.

Engine less carb — the small black bolt 'pinches' the carb in place.

CLUTCH FITTING

As already mentioned, there are two types of clutch fitting. The 'standard' type crank has threading along its length. The flywheel will be placed onto the crankshaft along with a slit taper collet. Then a clutch adaptor will bolt the flywheel to the crank, locking the flywheel in place. Often the crankshaft will need cutting down to stop the threaded section bottoming in the adaptor. To cut down the crank can be difficult, as it will be very hard. Firstly, completely wrap the engine in plastic, only allowing the end of the crank to stick out — it is most important that no metal filings find their way into the engine. Cut the crankshaft using a metal grinding disc. This can also be done on an ordinary grind wheel by carefully grinding away the crank until it is in two. Be very careful not to allow the engine to get covered in filings. Once the crank is cut, clean up any burrs. The flywheel can now be fitted to the engine. Hold the aluminium flywheel in soft jaws in a vice. Do up the adaptor with a ring spanner very tight. Nip the adaptor so that it pulls the flywheel properly onto the crankshaft.

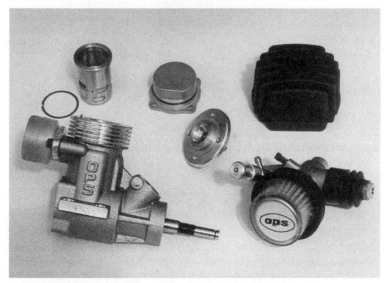

All the internals that make up a modern 3.5cc engine.

The second type of crankshaft — the 'SG' type — is much simpler. Again, a tapered collet is used but a simple nut runs down the thread to hold on the flywheel. This is tightened up the same as an adaptor. Follow the instructions given in your kit. If you need to cut down the clutch shoes, use a sharp knife and keep all cuts square to the shoes. It is important that, in two or three shoe clutches, all the shoes are the same, in weight and size, so they will grip at the same time. Once the clutch is fitted, the ballraces or needle roller bearings must be fitted next.

These bearings must be lubricated. Use a thick graphite grease, as this tends to stay on the bearings even at high 'Revs per Minute' (RPM). Once the bearings are fitted, the clutch drum can be placed on. These are usually held on with 'C' clips. Make sure the 'C' clip fits on securely and is not loose.

Manifold fitted to the engine via a rubber 'O' ring and spring.

EXHAUST FITTING

There are two main types of manifold used to remove the exhaust gases from the engine to the exhaust. One type uses a rubber mounted joint held in place by an exhaust spring. These are very simple to fit and work very well. No problems should be found fitting these although, if the manifold should need cutting down, make sure all sharp edges are removed with a file.

The second type of manifold bolts directly onto the crankcase of the engine. These need to be fitted correctly to avoid the vibrations making them fall off. Smear both faces of the manifold and crankcase with a small amount of silicone rubber. Put a mild loctite onto the screws which hold the manifold on. Do the screws up tightly in gradual steps so that the manifold is pulled down squarely. Allow the loctite and silicon to set completely before use. When fitting an exhaust pipe to a manifold, always use a high quality silicon tube. Try to use the braided type — these are more expensive but last longer. Secure the silicon tubing to the pipes with large tie-wraps. Always mount the silencer to the car securely.

Conrod and big end — note crankshaft is ground for balancing.

The carburettor in most engines is clamped in via a pinch bolt. Before placing the carb into the engine, smear a small amount of silicon rubber around the carb. Then place it in the crankcase and, using loctite, bolt it in place. Most carburettors have a rubber boot on the side. These can often be tie-wrapped in place, stopping any dirt getting behind them.

IC engine liner or cylinder made from brass and then chromed.

One of the most important items on any car engine is the filter. The air filter must be securely mounted to the carburettor. Clean both surfaces with motor cleaning spray. This will allow a seal between the rubber air filter and the carburettor. Make sure a good quality tie-wrap holds the filter on as near to the base of the carb as possible. Always fit a suitable filter into the fuel line. As with the air filter, this will also extend the life of your engine.

The engine will be mounted into the car via a set of engine mounts. The four bolts which hold the engine to the blocks must be secured with loctite. This is an area of great vibration, and the bolts will come undone if care is not taken to make sure they stay tight. At this stage, you should check the backplate screws and the head screws. Make sure you have a good quality screwdriver which fits the screws perfectly. If your engine uses allen screws, make sure your allen key is new and that is has no burrs.

IN THE CAR

When fitting the engine in the car, make sure that the gear mesh is correctly lined up. If not, the clutch belt will overheat and the possibility of a stripped gear will be greatly increased. Again, check the air filter to make sure it is safely secured. Check all fuel lines to make sure there are no kinks in the line, and keep them well tucked away from any gears or shafts. The smallest 'nick' in the fuel tube will stop the engine running and will be very difficult to find.

The throttle linkage must work smoothly and must not stick — the last thing you need is a car stuck on full throttle!

Rubber 'O' ring seals the carb to the engine crankcase.

FIRST RUN-UP

You will need a suitable 2 volt battery and plug lead. Also a 12 volt battery and a suitable electric starter. Firstly, remove the glowplug from the engine. Set the two main jets on the carburettor by screwing them both in, then turn them out three full turns. Fill the tank with fuel and, with the throttle fully open and the plug still out, turn the engine over in an anti-clockwise direction, when viewed from the clutch end of the crankshaft. Wait until you see fuel spurting from the plug hole. Return the throttle to shut and replace the glowplug. Put on the glowclip and turn over the engine. This should result in the engine starting. Do not over-rev the engine. Keep the revs down and allow the engine to bed in. The best way to run the engine in is to run the car on a flat piece of tarmac. Gently accelerate but do not reach full speed. Run around four tankfuls of fuel through the engine so that it will become run-in. On the fourth tankful the engine can be leaned out. Run the car up and down on full throttle, and gradually turn the main needle on the carburettor in a ¼ of a turn at a time until the speed of the car increases. At one point, the car will not want to run — it may even stop. This is too 'lean' so run the needle back out ¼ of a turn and run the car again. If it runs OK, then this is a good setting. If the car still wants to stop, give the needle a further ⅛ of a turn until the engine runs successfully.

Neat paper filter keeps the dirt out of the engine.

The second needle can now be set. This needle controls the acceleration. Again, we want to find a setting not too lean but just a little rich, i.e. too much fuel. Accelerate the car away from a standing start. If the car coughs and splutters and smokes a lot, this is too rich, so gradually turn the second needle in until the car pulls away cleanly. If, when you accelerate the car seems to want to stop, this is too lean, so turn the needle out to richen the engine.

The head holds the glowplug and aids cooling by a series of fins.

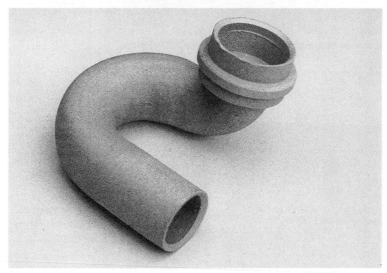

Cast manifolds are available to suit most applications.

Always try to run your engine a little rich (needles further out than in) — this will extend its life. Always check the fuel filter and air filter, as these can easily be blocked. The settings will need to be reset often due to weather conditions. Try to make all alterations in small steps, ¼ to ⅛ of a turn, as large adjustments are difficult to analyse and can cause problems. Change the plug in your engine regularly — every 30 minutes running is a good guide. If your engine seems to blow plugs, try to run it richer, as this adds to engine cooling.

A starter box makes life easy for starting IC engines.

11 ROAD HUGGING

All you have done so far is to build your car so that the suspension moves freely. To control the suspension, off-road cars use either springs, or a combination of springs and dampers. The whole idea of the suspension is to keep the wheels on the ground at all times. Cars are driven across very rough tracks, therefore the wheels cannot always be on the ground, but the suspension can be tuned to help the wheels stay on the ground and to make sure that the car does not bounce when it returns to the ground after leaping in the air. Suspension can also be altered to allow different handling characteristics, such as more or less steering.

As already stated, suspension arms should be made to pivot without any tightness. The damper and spring should do all the work. On kits that are just fitted with springs, very little can be done. The best answer to improve performance is to fit an oil-filled damper update kit. For cars already fitted with dampers, there is a set of rules to be followed to make sure you get the most from your car's suspension.

There are various grades of springs available. It is best to have maybe a maximum of three — soft, medium and hard. With this limited amount, confusion should not occur. The spring actually absorbs energy when the car hits a bump — this energy is then let out as the spring uncoils. This can send the car leaping off the ground. The damper slows down this unleashing of the spring and helps keep the wheels in contact with the ground. The idea is to adjust the springing and damping so that the car's chassis is suspended away from the ground and the damping is at its lightest, enabling the wheels to follow the surface without causing bouncing.

Selection of available tyres from PB Schumacher and Dynamite.

CAT tyres fitted to Brimod wheels.

DAMPERS

Almost all kits (1:10th and 1:8th) today feature oil-filled dampers. The damper consists of a shaft, cylinder and a piston. The shaft is connected to the suspension arm, the cylinder to the chassis. On the shaft is fixed a piston. The piston moves up and down with the suspension inside the oil-filled cylinder. The piston fits the cylinder snugly but has a series of holes that allow the oil to pass through. Different oils or sizes of holes allow the piston to move up and down at different rates, therefore adjusting the damping.

These dampers need to be assembled and filled with oil correctly if they are to work well. Most shock absorbers come with excellent instructions but a few tips may help in building them.

Always make sure that any oil seal rubbers do not get damaged during assembly. Clean all plastic parts thoroughly, making sure there is no moulding sprue on the pistons. Most dampers have a rubber diaphragm fitted in the top. This allows for the shaft entering the cylinder and helps keep the damping smooth. This should be fitted correctly and care taken not to crimp the edges during fitting. Silicon oils are the best available to use in suspension systems. They have a very stable constitution and are not effected by heat build up. Always ensure that you completely fill the dampers and do not allow any air bubbles, as this will cause unsteadiness in the car's handling. It is best to start with the car slightly underdamped as, when the vehicle is cold, this can tend to stiffen all the suspension components. It is impossible to give a damper setting, and only practice and experiment will give good results.

RIDE HEIGHT

Ride heights and spring stiffness are two different things. Your car should always use the softest springs possible without the car hitting the ground continuously. The ride height of the car should always be kept to a minimum, as this will allow the car to steer easily and will aid the general handling. Ride height is adjusted by collets which hold the spring position on the damper. These collets adjust the spring position and raise or lower where the car sits in relation to the ground.

TOE IN OR OUT?

Another section of your car's suspension that needs to be considered is 'toe in' on the front wheels. Most kits will tell you to have a touch of toe-in to keep the car stable in a straight line. This is good advice, although do not overdo the amount — 1-2° or 2-3mm on the track rods is plenty. On 4WD (four-wheel drive) cars, slightly less or almost parallel front wheels are more desirable.

Parma have produced these new tyres along CAT lines — this type of tyre is the most popular in use.

WHEELS AND TYRES

The wheels and tyres are the only contact with the ground your car should have, so, this is an important area for consideration. What is most important is that the tyres remain squarely fixed onto the wheels.

Rallycross cars often need their tyres glued to the rim. Take the rim and roughen the surface to be glued with a coarse sand paper (P60). When the wheel is roughened, clean the wheel with motor spray so that it is absolutely grease-free. Clean the tyre also with motor spray. Often black rubber will come off onto the rag — this is OK and shows that the tyre is clean.

Place the tyre onto the rim without gluing. Make sure that the tyre is on squarely all the way round. This can be done by placing the wheel on the car and spinning it. When the tyre is on square, start gluing in a circular motion. Lift up the tyre slightly from the rim and squeeze super glue down the gap. Make sure glue runs all round the tyre on both sides. Wipe any excess glue off with a rag. Some super glues can be cured with a setting agent. If you do this, make sure it is in a ventilated area, as the gases given off can be dangerous. When super gluing, always be careful — super glue tends to stick to fingers better than anything else!

The Mardave Meteor fitted with its angry-looking directional tyres — facing forward.

Various grades of oil are available to change the stiffness of the dampers.

Keep the suspension soft — this way it will soak up the bumps.

BOLT 'EM ON

Some 1:10 kits use a two piece wheel which bolts together, clamping the tyre in place. This is a simple idea that works well, but make sure the tyre is trapped evenly all round the rim.

By far the most popular method is the wheels which hold the tyres without glue in a slot. These tyres are easy to fit, and are easily removed to replace with new ones. These are featured in almost all 1:10 kits.

Kyosho Lazer has a series of positions to connect the damper.

Most cars have a small amount of camber change, ie. the wheels tip in at the top as the suspension is pushed down.

Damper shaft and piston. Note sealing 'O' ring on end cap.

TYRE CHOICE

Whatever your kit comes with should be used. Tyres rarely wear out on grass or mud, but obviously wear rapidly on tarmac or concrete. If you do practise on tarmac, keep a set of old tyres handy — don't wear out new tyres for nothing.

The damping should be kept to a minimum to allow the suspension to move freely.

Generally pin spike tyres are the most popular, giving good grip and wear rates. Sand tyres are also available but are less popular.

For 2WD (two-wheel drive) cars, ribbed front tyres are used. There is a large selection of tyres available, and these can be selected for giving varying degrees of steering.

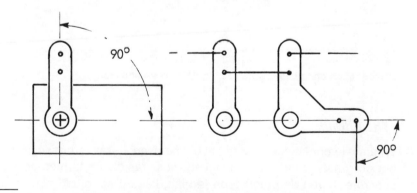

Keep all steering bellcranks at 90 degrees to one another.

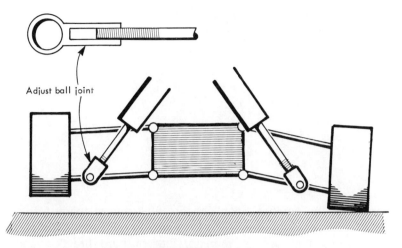

Adjust ball joint

Adjust shock absorbers to give equal ground clearance.

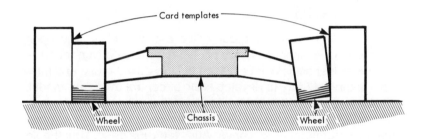

Card templates

Wheel   Chassis   Wheel

Use cardboard plates to set camber on wheels.

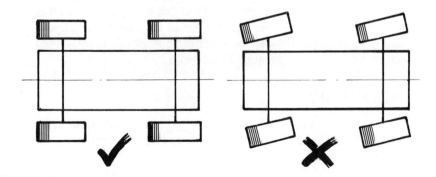

12 GET THE BUG

Now that the car has been chosen, built and is ready for its maiden voyage, there is still a long way to go. Before you can experience the joys of winning, lots of hard practice and developing of skills are needed.

WHERE TO START

Anyone can drive a radio controlled car around a large open space. What is needed is a set of obstacles to be driven round — this gives a specific point at which to slow down, brake and turn. This is the only way to develop skills of control over your model.

When you start, it is best not to have an audience. Find somewhere away from the public and animals and have a quiet practise around a set of cones. After ten runs or so, you should be able to keep the car running smoothly (without stopping) around the cones. Make sure that you remain standing in one place — don't follow the car as, when you go racing, you'll be expected to stand on a rostrum with all the other drivers. At this point, try not to let the car's performance take too much of your attention. It doesn't matter how fast it goes at this point — just get as much time practising as possible.

YOUR FIRST MEETING

After plenty of practice in the back garden or the local open space, you're bound to want to have a go on a purpose-built, real racing circuit.

The best procedure to follow is to attend your local club to see how the racing is run, in advance of your own first race meeting. Turning up on time and having the necessary equipment (like a 12 volt battery) is all part of a successful first meeting. If you attend a local club, make a point of finding out how much the entry fee is and whether your car is eligible for racing. Also, it often helps if you have a spare set of radio frequency crystals as, at race meetings, making sure everyone is on different frequencies is part of the procedure.

Out on the track — take things easy at first and learn the circuit gradually.

Two-speed gearbox for a Kyosho Burns — the ultimate racing accessory.

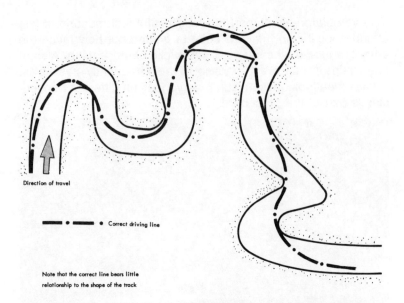

Direction of travel

●—●—● Correct driving line

Note that the correct line bears little
relationship to the shape of the track

Maybe a slightly exaggerated line but this really would be the fastest way
through the corners — note how different the correct line is to the track
shape.

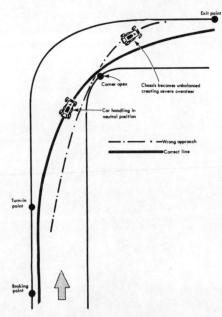

Exit point

Corner apex

Chassis becomes unbalanced
creating severe oversteer

Car handling in
neutral position

●—●—● Wrong approach

Correct line

Turn-in
point

Braking
point

This is the quickest way through a 90 degree corner although it must be
remembered to be slow into the corner and fast out.

When you first hit the track don't expect to be the fastest car on the circuit! Firstly 'feel' your way around the track at half speed — if you get all the way round without an accident you'll be doing well! Gradually speed up but at all times keep your driving smooth and flowing.

Most manufacturers have a range of racing tune-up modifications.

The quickest way round the corners is to take the longest route at the highest speed. This keeps the car going as straight as possible and therefore the speed is kept up. The actual position at which to turn is more easily described in diagram on p106.

Basically, the corners should be made into a continuous flow — no sharp movements should be made. The best drivers in the world become so, apart from their ability to drive quickly, by being able to read the track and other drivers in front of them. When coming up to slower cars, instead of making last minute dives at the back of other drivers, it is best to tuck in behind the car and wait for a clear opportunity in which a safe overtaking manoeuvre can be made. Time lost being placed back on the circuit by a marshall can rarely be made up by driving quickly.

Don't forget to place your numbers on the bodyshell.

Most races are started from a straight line-up.

Always walk the circuit before you drive your car round it. It is only by walking and looking that you will see jumps and bumps that are invisible from the drivers' rostrum.

Once you're well into racing, an airbrush system makes bodyshell painting easy.

Drivers' rostrums are usually high — be careful if you're in a rush!

Whatever form of car racing you drive in, good driving technique is the key to success. The most expensive motor chassis or tyres are useless unless their advantage can be used in a smooth and professional way.

Good driving can only be explained in strict terms. What is far more educational is to watch other drivers at your local club — try to watch the guys who win regularly and see how they take the corners. They are probably not the most spectacular, but almost certainly they are the smoothest!

The ideal end — being presented with a trophy!

APPENDIX ONE

1990 1:10th OFF-ROAD CAR RACING RULES

1. APPEARANCE

1.1 Cars entered for off-road competitions should be reasonable representations of the style of full-size cars generally accepted as being suitable for rallycross, rallying, trail or desert races.

1.2 Open roll cage style cars will be permitted to compete if the entrant can supply proof that the car is closely based on a full-size example.

1.3 The roll cage of any open cage car must enclose all drive and guidance equipment.

1.4 Any commercially available 1:10th scale body shell may be used other than open-wheeled Formula 1 type shells or sports racing shells.

1.5 In the case of open cockpit cars a realistic driver figure must be included.

1.6 All cars must make suitable arrangements for racing numbers to be displayed facing to the front and one each side.

1.7 No car may be raced without a bodyshell being securely fitted at all times.

1.8 When initially entered in a meeting the body must be neatly finished.

2. GENERAL CONSTRUCTION RULES

2.1 No car shall be constructed so as to be dangerous or to damage other competitors cars.

2.2 The overall width of the front bumper must not exceed the overall width of the front of the car including wheels. It must not be less than 60% of the width. The bumper must be constructed of a resilient material such as plastic or rubber, minimum thickness is 2.5mm and edges must be rounded.

2.3 Dimensions must conform to the following:

Maximum length — 460mm (including bumpers).

Maximum width — 250mm at any point of suspension travel, in a vertical plain.

Minimum weight — 52oz 2WD and 56oz 4WD complete and ready to race, excluding any lap scoring equipment.

2.4 The chassis can be made of any type of material and can be of any thickness.

2.5 There are no limitations on the steering.

2.6 There are no limitations on the suspension.

2.7 Any type of speed controller may be used, but it must be contained within the car and not protrude through the bodyshell.

2.8 Drive batteries must conform to the following:
The cars will be driven by a maximum of six cells, only Sub-C sized Nicads are approved. The size of the individual cells, rated at 1.2v nominal is 23mm diameter, 43mm length nominal. Entrants must be prepared to open packs on demand of the race scrutineer to demonstrate the eligibility of the cells.

2.9 The radio box is not mandatory but is recommended.

2.10 There are no limitations on gears.

2.11 Differentials are allowed.

2.12 Ball races may be used.

2.13 Wheels and tyres must conform as follows:
No form of metal or plastic spike tubes or anything similar shall be attached to the tyres. The maximum diameter allowed is 90mm front and rear. Any combination of comercially available wheels and tyres may be used.

2.14 Motors fall into two classes: Standard and Modified, and must conform to the following:

Standard Class

i) Only nationally commercially available motors may be used.

ii) The maximum retail cost of motors not to exceed £15.00. Any options such as tweaking etc. must be included within price. Any Standard motor offered with options above price limit will be deemed illegal.

iii) Only unopened, unmodified, permanently factory sealed motors may be used.

iv) In the case of open endbell motor brushes and springs may be replaced with original specification parts.

v) Only one drive motor may be used.

vi) Windings — Minimum of 27 turns of 22 gauge wire only, single wind.

vii) Only 540 size motors allowed.

viii) Only motors approved by the 1:10th Committee offer approval by the Eligibility Officer will be accepted for use at BRCA sanctioned meetings.

ix) Only plain bearings allowed, ball races may not be fitted.

Modified Class

i) Only motors with a retail cost of £40.00 and under may be used.

ii) Only one drive motor may be used.

iii) No rare earth i.e. cobalt magnets allowed.

iv) Only 540 size motors allowed.

2.15 Four wheel drive is allowed until such time that the Committee feels a separate class is justified.

2.16 At the organiser's or BRCA's discretion any motor may be stripped or, if three separate protests are registered providing £5.00 is put forward in each case. If the motor is found to be legal the competitor will be reimbursed.

2.17 Any new Nicads or motors (Standard or Modified) must be approved by the BRCA Eligibility Officer, published in Circuit Chatter and be commercially available for three months prior to being approved for use.

3. 380 Class

3.1 Rules for the appearance of the 380 class are the same as for the 540 class rules 1.1 to 1.8

3.2 General construction rules for the 380 class cars are the same as for the 540 class with the following exceptions:

i) These cars shall be commercially available 380 kits only.

ii) They can only incorporate the kit supplied chassis.

iii) Only the ball joints, track rods and servo saver may be altered in the steering equipment.

iv) The gears may be replaced with stronger alternatives and the ratio altered.

v) Only manufacturer's differentials are allowed.

vi) The suspension has to be as per the kit with the additions of dampers only.

vii) Any 380 motors are allowed at a retail cost of £6.00 maximum.

viii) Protective covers may be fitted to waterproof the car.

4. R/C EQUIPMENT

4.1 Only legally approved radio controlled frequencies may be used.

4.2 Entrants should ideally be prepared to use any legal frequency, but in any event should have at least two frequencies to that entered available.

4.3 Power supply for the transmitter must not exceed the designed voltage for the transmitter.

4.4 Reversed crystals are prohibited and their use will result in disqualification (all legal frequencies to be listed).

5. TRACK

5.1 Corner cutting must be discouraged by placing markings and barriers.

5.2 Start and finish lines must be marked

5.3 Tracks to be at least 8 feet wide, but narrower sections may be included (chicanes) and the start straight should have no obstructions in its length.

5.4 The start straight should be 10m long.

5.5 Track should be laid out so that there are no hidden areas when viewed from the drivers' rostrum area.

5.6 Adequate protection should be provided for spectators.

5.7 Staggered starts at one second intervals should be used at all National and International meetings during qualifying heats. After the first round of heats, starting is based on finishing positions of previous heat.

5.7a All National and International finals should have staggered starts at one metre intervals and two rows of cars. Pole position to choose side of grid.

6. RACE PROCEDURES & CHAMPIONSHIP PROCEDURES

6.1 All heats and finals shall be of the same duration.

6.2 Race duration shall be a minimum of 5 mins.

6.3 A maximum of 2 minutes warning will be given prior to the commencement of the race.

6.4 Any car jumping the start signal will be penalised.

6.5 Qualifying heats shall consist of a maximum of ten cars.

6.6 Finals shall consist of a maximum of eight cars.

6.7 There should be a minimum of six cars per race starting heat.

6.8 Finals shall be of the A to Z style. 100 points for a win downwards, 1 point for the 100th place.

6.9 380 Motor Finals as per 540.

6.10 National Championships to be raced to Modified rules only. Championship to consist of 7 rounds per class.

6.11 British National Championships to consist of two separate classes run at separate meetings i.e. 2WD Modified (front or rear WD only) or 4WD Modified (max of four driven wheels only).

6.12 All national Championship rounds and Regional finals must have individual lap times of all competitors.

6.13 Any car receiving assistance of an unfair nature (i.e. being pushed) to get to the finish line will be disqualified.

6.14 1:10th Off Road Section to provide an automatic lap counting system at all National Championship rounds and Regional finals. Drivers to be levied to pay for the system.

6.15 Circuit to be closed for practice the day prior to National Championship meetings.

6.16 All National Championship heats and finals must use a grid start.

6.17 Only BRCA members to score points towards Regional Championship.

6.18 All "A" Finals to be run over three legs, results should be decided by the position of each driver's best two races. Any ties to be decided by the fastest time in the two qualifying legs.

6.18a Points scored in the three leg "A" final should be as follows:

1st — 10 points	3rd — 8 points	5th — 6 points	7th — 4 points
2nd — 9 points	4th — 7 points	6th — 5 points	8th — 3 points

6.19 Top twenty drivers from previous year's Championship to be split amongst the top six heats.

6.20 i) Entries to the National Junior Championship should be through qualification through Regional Summer Leagues.

ii) Championships to be split into two classes

(a) Under 13 years of age on 1st April.

(b) 13 years of age to under 17 years on 1st April.

iii) Separate finals for both age groups at the Championships.

iv) Top five from each age group to qualify for Championship.

7. SCORING

7.1 100 points shall be awarded for a win. 99 for 2nd place etc (this only applies to BRCA members at points meetings).

7.2 Points shall be awarded on finishing positions in finals. 100 points for A Final 1st place. 99 points for A Final 2nd place and so on down.

7.3 Scores to count towards the Championship 50% of meetings plus 1.

7.4 Driver with highest points total is the winner.

7.5 BRCA to appoint two referees at all National Championship rounds to oversee driving manners. Referees need not be BRCA Sectional Committee.

8. INTERNATIONAL CHAMPIONSHIPS

8.1 Any driver wishing to compete in World or European Championship events must advise in writing with a £20.00 fee to the Teams Officer by the previous AGM.

8.2 European Championship team to be selected from the previous year's National Championship results, and to be selected from the relevant class championship.

8.3 World Championship team to be selected from previous year's National Championship result and to be selected from the relevant class championship.

9. REGIONAL CHAMPIONSHIPS

9.1 Regional rounds should not be held on the same day as a National or International meeting.

9.2 Individual Regions to decide the rules that the Championships should be run to (Standard or Modified). Regional finals to be run to Standard rules.

1:10th OFF ROAD — RACE PROCEDURE
Set out below are some points on race procedure at BRCA sanctioned National Meetings:-

1(a) Appoint a Race Director.

1(b) The decisions of the Race Director are final.

2. Class of racing to be made clear e.g. Standard or Modified.

3. Number of round to be run — minimum 3.

4. Duration of heats — recommended 5 mins.

5. Operation of timing system, inform drivers if they have to finish lap etc.

6. Start/Finish signals.

7. Marshalling duties — penalties for not marshalling.

8. Driving standards — penalties can be given for the following:
(a) collision with "on line" car.   (b) T-boning.
(c) Reversing out into on-coming cars.   (d) Erratic or inconsiderate driving.

9. Unsportsmanlike behaviour — a competitor can be disqualified from a meeting for consistent use of foul language or aggressive behaviour.

10. Position of site facilities i.e. toilets, refreshments etc.

11. Scrutineering Bay — please note a set of scales and a box conforming to the regulation dimensions is advisable.

12. Preference will be given to BRCA members at sanctioned meetings, up until the official closing date.

13. The BRCA Committee would like to see a discount given to BRCA members at sanctioned National meetings of 50p.

14. Any competitor found using illegal equipment may at the Race Director's discretion be disqualified from the meeting and subject to appearing before the 1:10th Off Road Committee may be disqualified from participating in any other BRCA sanctioned event.

14(a) Subject to the findings of the Committee the BRCA may take repercussions against the manufacturer of any illegal equipment.

15. The Committee recommends the following allocation of trophies: A and B Finals — all drivers receive trophy. C to E finals top three in each. All other Finals top two in each. A trophy for the top qualified (FTD).

16. Provision should be made for a member to enter his number with his entry and result for points calculation purposes.

17. Meeting results to be forwarded to the Calender/Points Co-ordinator within 7 days.

18. Please check that a Club is insured for the meeting and that non-BRCA members are covered.

19. All meetings should be finished by 6.30pm.

APPENDIX TWO

1990 1:8th OFF-ROAD CAR RACING RULES

1. **Aims**

   To provide a uniform format for 1:8th scale off-road racing cars to compete with one another on an open National basis. The intention is to encompass all commercially available 1:8th scale cars, yet still encourage invention and innovation with the great aim of developing the hobby by allowing 1-off home constructed cars, and modifications of kit products.

2. **Technical Specification**
   i) General dimensions
   (a) Overall length 730 mm Maximum.
   (b) Overall width 310mm Maximum.
   (c) Wheelbase 270-330 mm.
   (d) Overall height measured from the ground including rollbar at full suspension compression 250mm Maximum. (This measurement does not include the receiver aerial).
   (e) The car shall be measured for width by placing it on a baseboard equipped with two side rails of 20mm height spaced 310mm apart constructed in such a way that the car can roll freely between them. Baseboard and rails must be constructed of high quality board suitably stiffened to prevent distortion. The car must roll freely between the side rails with any steerable wheels set in the straight ahead position irrespective of the compression, extension or roll angle of the suspension.
   (f) The car shall be measured for length and height in a similarly constructed box of internal dimensions 730 x 310mm, which includes provision for checking maximum height.
   (g) The measurement of the wheelbase may be made by simple measurement of axle centre distances with the suspension in any position. Race Directors should be prepared to make more exact checks in case of doubt or protest. It is suggested that the wheels are removed and the wheel spindles placed on vee blocks whilst accurate measurements are made.
   (h) It is the responsibility of the driver to ensure that his car complies with the regulations at all times that it is on the track. Race organisers may check any car for compliance with the regulations at any time during a race meeting.
   (i) If a car is found to exceed the limits of dimensions on checking immediately after a race, positive proof of race damage may prevent disqualification.
   ii) Engines
   (a) Internal combustion engines with a maximum capacity of 3.5 cubic centimetres.
   (b) Fuel tank capacity 125 cubic centimetres maximum including all piping tubes and filter up to the carburettor.
   (c) Exhaust noise level should not exceed 80Db at 10 metres.
   iii) Tyres
   All tyres must be black, with the exception of side wall lettering.
   iv) Wings
   A wing of maximum overall size 217mm length and 77mm width may be fitted.

3. Appearance

(a) Cars shall be a reasonable representation of the style of car used for off-road, desert or trial racing.

(b) Full bodyshells of saloon style are permitted, but they may only be trimmed to expose 50% of the tyres at full suspension depression. If such bodyshells are fitted, provision for trimming shall be as in EFRA section viii. 5.5d.

(c) Where a roll cage is fitted, an open wheel style bodyshell must be fitted underneath the cage, so designed as to enclose R/C equipment and fuel tank with sufficient front and side areas as to allow clear display of racing numbers.

(d) Openings may be cut in the shell to allow access to fuel filler, switch and engine adjustments. Clearance around such items shall be kept to a minimum.

(e) Bodyshells as described in (c) need not conform to scale but should conform to the provisions of EFRA section viii. 5.5a. Acceptance of a saloon bodyshell by another EFRA or BRCA section shall be deemed to imply approval by the Rally Cross section for racing purposes.

4. Radio Control Equipment

a) It is the responsibility of all drivers to ensure that their equipment does not cause interference to others, and that his receiver is not faulty.

b) Only legally approved frequencies are to be used.

c) Drivers must be able to provide at least one alternative frequency.

d) Flags shall not be used on aerials during races.

e) A frequency "pegboard" system shall be used at all times.

f) Under no circumstances shall a transmitter be taken onto the track.

g) All frequency changes must be approved by the Race Director.

h) It is not permitted to add any additional nicad or dry cell batteries to a transmitter either internally or externally to raise the designed supply voltage above the original manufacturer's design specification i.e. a six cell transmitter may not be fitted with more than 6 cells, either ni-cad or dry cell, also any 8 cell transmitter may not be fitted with more than eight cells etc.

5. Scrutineering

a) Only cars which conform to the construction rules may compete.

b) Only one entry per driver will be accepted.

c) Cars may be inspected at any time during the race and after the final.

d) Any part of the car may be substituted during a race, except the chassis or chassis rails, these may be changed with the approval of the Race Director.

e) Damage caused during a race will not be penalised except in the case of excessive noise from the engine or the total loss of the bodyshell.

6. Concours D' Elegance

a) A Concours may be held before the start of racing.

b) The body and chassis of cars judged for Concours must take part in the race.

c) The Concours judge may if he wishes take into account the chassis preparation.

7. Entrance Requirements

a) Entry forms for BRCA Championship Meetings should be distributed via Circuit Chatter.

b) Closing date for entries should be not more than 10 days before the race.

c) In the event of over-subscription of a meeting, the organiser shall accept entries in the order in which he receives them, using the postmark as the date of entry.

d) The organiser should appoint the following officials.

    i) Race Director — in control of all racing.

    ii) Referee — in control of driving standards interference decisions, protests, rule application, etc. scrutineering.

    iii) Chief Timekeeper — in control of time-keeping.

e) Entrants should be required to provide proof of BRCA membership.

f) In the case of late arrival to a race, all properly entered drivers will be accepted until the end of qualifying heats.

8. Race Procedure

a) A driver's briefing must be held by the Race Director, Referee and Timekeeper before racing starts.

b) The driver's briefing should include guidance on the following:
   i) Starts and Finish.
   ii) Refuelling, marshalling, repairs, transmitters.
   iii) Protest procedure.
   iv) Driver's conduct.

c) All qualifying heats shall be of 5 minutes duration. Four rounds of qualification heats shall be run for all drivers, unless the entry exceeds 56 competitors. When the number of heats will be reduced to 3.

d) A maximum number of 8 cars per qualifying heat.

e) Qualification for finals shall be determined by each drivers single best heat time. In the event of a tie, the second best heat time shall be used.

f) There shall be a period of 3 minutes from the finish of a heat to the start of the following heat. An audible warning shall be given 1 minute before the start of all heats.

9. Start Procedure

a) At the start of all races, all cars are to be held on the start line by the mechanics.

b) The starter shall indicate to the mechanic to release the cars and step back 1 pace, and all cars shall remain stationary.

c) The starter shall hold cars stationary at the start for a maximum of 10 seconds.

d) Any car which moves forward, and crosses outside the start box may be subject to a penalty.

e) The starter may call a re-start if he cannot identify the car(s) that made a false start.

f) A start box for each car must be marked out of no less than 1 metre in length and 0.5 metres in width.

g) Le Mans type starts will be used for all main finals. Cars to be placed along main straight with at least 5 metres between each car, where track does not allow for this amount of spacing the whole of the main straight must be used.

h) A start marshall to be used at all times to indicate to mechanics when to release cars.

10. Finish

a) A car will be deemed to have finished the race the first time it crosses the finish line after the expiry of the duration of any heat or final.

b) Only cars on the track at the time of the finish shall be given a split time i.e. the total laps completed at the finish shall be the time, with no time for last lap.

c) No car may be pushed over the finish line.

11. Race Interruption

a) The Race Director may decide to interrupt the race due to adverse weather.

b) If all competitors have not had one heat in the dry, but all have had one in the wet only, the wet heat results will be counted.

c) If more than half the final has been run and the race has to be stopped the positions at the time of interruption will be the result.

d) In the case of a heat being interrupted the entire heat will be re-run.

12. Protests

a) The organiser may correct anything deemed necessary without a protest.

b) All protests must be made in writing to the Referee, together with a £10 deposit. If the protest is upheld this money will be reimbursed.

c) Protests must be made within 5 minutes of the results in question.

d) Protests regarding the legality of cars must be made in writing together with the fee to the Referee.

13. Penalties and Black Flag

a) The Race Director may at his discretion penalise competitors by disqualification or loss of best heat time for the following infringements:-

i.   Disregard of official decisions.
ii. Corner cutting.
iii. Unauthorised use of transmitters.
iv. Incorrect use of pits
v.   Repairs or refuelling on the track.
vi. Unauthorised frequency changes. Illegal frequencies.
vii. Unauthorised changing of chassis plate/rails.
viii. Cars not conforming to regulations.
ix. Non-sporting behaviour, bad language.
b)   A car which is black-flagged must be removed from the track immediately. A car may be black-flagged for the following infringements:-
i.   Deliberately impeding the progress of other cars.
ii. Non-sporting racing.
iii. Driving in a dangerous manner.
iv. Cars in an undriveable or dangerous condition. (These cars may restart after repairs, with the Race Director/Referee's permission).
v.   Cars losing their bodies or whose silencers become ineffective. (These cars may restart after the necessary repairs).

14. **Finals & National Championship Series**
   (a) There will only be one class of National Championship unrestricted. This will include both 4WD and 2WD cars to run as one class, there will be no separate restricted class.
   (b) At the termination of the qualifying rounds the top 40 qualifiers will be placed in order, this will then be used to compile four finals of the cars in each, run in the sequence D. C. B and A. A minimum of four cars is required to constitute a final.
   (c) A £2.50 levy over and above the entry fee shall be collected by the organising club from each competitor at all National and International meetings to fund automatic timing equipment purchase and maintenance. This levy to be reviewed annually at Conference.
   (e) The annual National Championship two day meeting shall be modelled on, but not necessarily identical to EFRA rules. Qualification shall consist of a minimum of four 5 minute rounds, the top 10 qualifiers will qualify. 5 into each Semi Final and the fastest five drivers will qualify from each Sub final race. All sub finals will be of 20 minutes duration, and the Final shall be of 45 minutes duration. Only drivers qualifying on the day allocated for qualification shall race in the following day's sub-finals. The results of the meeting will be used to allocate championship points to the top 40 finalists using lap scores to differentiate between identical placings in similar finals. In the event of a tie, qualification times will be used.
   (f) 75% of championship meetings that take place will count towards overall placings rounded up or down to the nearest whole number.
   (g) If any driver withdraws from the meeting before the final he is qualifying for is run, his place will remain open.
   (h) Tied championship positions shall be resolved, by firstly comparing results of discarded meetings and secondly by the number of 1st. 2nds etc places as may be required.
   (i) BRCA Championship points will be awarded at a British Grand Prix and count towards the BRCA National Championship Series. British drivers will be awarded points from 1st to 40th place disregarding results gained by other foreign drivers.

16. **Track and Safety**
   a) Spectators and marshalls should be protected from the risk of being hit by cars.
   b) Track markers should be such that they minimise the risks of cars becoming airborne.
   c) Track markers and tracks should be designed so as to minimise risk of damage to cars.

APPENDIX THREE

USEFUL ADDRESSES

British radio Car Association (BRCA)
Secretary — Alan Harman
C/O Radio Control Model Cars
Magazine
Argus Specialist Publications
Argus House
Boundary Way
Hemel Hempstead
Herts HP2 7ST
Tel: 0442 66551

MAP Insurance
Argus Specialist Publications
Argus House
Boundary Way
Hemel Hempstead
Herts HP2 7ST
Tel: 0442 66551

Radio Control Model Cars Magazine
Editor — Alan Harman
Argus Specialist Publications
Argus House
Boundary Way
Hemel Hempstead
Herts HP2 7ST
Tel: 0442 66551

International Federation of Model
Auto Racing (IFMAR)
President — Ted Longshaw
Beech Tree House
Westhill
Downe
Orpington
Kent

European Federation of Radio
Operated Model Automobiles (EFRA)
Secretary — Fer Van Helden
Jadelaan 20
NL 3523
CV Utrecht

ROAR & FEMCA
(American Associations)
Mike Reedy
3585 Cadillac Avenue
Costa Mesa
CA 92626
USA
Tel: (714) 850 9342

APPENDIX FOUR

UK/USA IMPORTERS AND MANUFACTURERS

UK

AMERANG LTD
Commerce Way, Lancing, Sussex
BN15 8TE.
Tel: 0903 765496.

HELGER RACING (Parma Products)
R/O 25 Horsecroft Road, The Pinnacles,
Harlow, Essex CM19 5BH.
Tel: 0279 641097

P B RACING PRODUCTS LTD
Downley Road, Havant, Hampshire
PO9 2NJ.
Tel: 0705 492310 or 492311.

RIKO INTERNATIONAL LTD
(Tamiya Products)
13-15a High Street, Hemel Hempstead,
Herts HP1 3AD.
Tel: 0442 61721.

RIPMAX LTD (Kyosho Products)
Ripmax Corner, Green Street, Enfield,
Essex.
Tel: 01 804 8272.

SCHUMACHER RACING PRODUCTS
LTD
Hanson Business Park, 71-73 Tenter
Road, Moulton Park, Northampton
NN3 1AX.
Tel: 0604 790770

MACGREGOR INDUSTRIES
(JR Products)
Canal Estate, Langley, Berks.
Tel: 0753 49111.

INTRONICS
Claerwen, Bexhill Road, Pevensey, East
Sussex.
Tel: 0323 763688.

SRM RACING
140 West Street, Fareham, Hants PO16.
Tel: 0329 234262.

LASER PRODUCTS
Lesro Models, Stony Lane, Christchurch,
Dorset BH23 7LQ.
Tel: 0202 476902.

DEMON PRODUCTS
P O Box 12, Aldershot, Hants.
Tel: 0252 343132.

NORAK PRODUCTS
Central Models, 1684 Bristol Road South,
Birmingham.
Tel: 021 453 9631.

SPEED MASTER
30 Mancroft Road, Caddington, Luton
LU1 4EL.

KO PRODUCTS
Penn Models, 317 Penn Road
Wolverhampton
WV4 5QF.

SANWA PRODUCTS
Irvine Engines, Unit 2 Brunswick Industrial
Park, Brunswick Way, London.
Tel: 01 361 1123/4.

FASTLINE
50 Nunnery Road, Frome, Somerset

SANYO BATTERIES
Phil Greeno Models, 9 Village Way East,
Rayners Lane, Middx.
Tel: 01 866 7770.

FREWER PRODUCTS
TMS Models, Deansfield Mills, Asquith
Avenue, Morley, Leeds.
Tel: 0532 523023.

FLEET LTD
Fleet Control Systems, 47 Fleet Road,
Fleet, Hants.
Tel: 0252 615011.

TRINITY MOTORS
Lesro Models, Stony Lane, Christchurch.
Tel: 0202 476902.

NOSRAM ELECTRONICS
10 Bronsil Drive, Malvern.
Tel: 0684 567655.

MUGEN LTD
Elite Models, 159 Newgate Lane,
Mansfield, Notts.
Tel: 0623 36062.

TEAM LOSI
CML Distribution, 1684 Bristol Road
South, Birmingham.
Tel: 021 453 9631.

MANTUA MODELS
Windsor Models, 45 Albany Road,
Windsor.
Tel: 0753 856321.

PUMA RACING MODELS
The Barn, Moat House Works, Alcester.
Tel: 0789 765496.

USA

AEROTREND PRODUCTS
31 Nichols Street, Ansonia,
CT 06401-1106.
Tel: (203) 734-0600.
Products: Many Radio Control accessories
for cars, boats, planes, helicopters, including "BlueLine" tubing, many size battery
packs, bearing kits for many R/C cars.

AIRTRONICS INC
11 Autry, Irvine, CA 92718.
Products: R/C airplanes, R/C systems and
accessories.

ARISTO-CRAFT/POLK'S MODEL CRAFT
HOBBIES
346 Bergen Avenue, Jersey City,
NJ 07304.
Tel: (201) 332-8100.
Products: Manufacture R/C systems,
chargers, speed controls, ARF planes,
boats and cars. Also produce wood ship
models and parts.

ASSOCIATED ELECTRICS INC
3585 Cadillac Avenue, Costa Mesa,
CA 92626.
Tel: (714) 850-9342.
Products: Manufacture and sell world
championship winning R/C race cars like
RC10, RC10L, RC12L, RC500 and sell
Yokomo YZ10 and all spare parts and
accessories.

ASTRO FLIGHT INC
13311 Beach Avenue, Marine del Ray,
CA 90292.
Tel: (213) 821-6242.
Products: Electric motors, battery
chargers, Ni-Cad batteries, accessories
and electric airplane kits. High Quality
manufactured products.

CRP/CUSTOM RACING PRODUCTS
3250 El Camino Real-B3, Atascadero,
CA 93422.
Tel: (805) 466-6945.
Products: Aftermarket parts and accessor-
ies for 1/10 scale on and off-road cars.

CERMARK ELECTRONIC AND MODEL
SUPPLY
107 Edward Avenue, PO Box 2406,
Fullerton, CA 92633.
Tel: (714) 680-5888.
Products: Ready to fly airplane, glider,
Sanyo Ni-Cad battery and battery packs.
Battery charger, heat shrink tubing, radio
connectors. Electric 10:1 car and
accessories.

CONDOR R/C SPECIALITIES
1733 Monrovia Avenue G, Costa Mesa,
CA 92627.
Tel: (714) 642-8020.
Products: Speciality R/C equipment and
accessories bridging the gap between
normal recreational R/C and industrial
RPV, UAV, robotics applications.

COX HOBBIES INC
Div Aeromil Engineering Co, 1525,
E Warner Avenue, Santa Ana, CA 92705.
Tel: (714) 546-2551.
Products: Beginner-level ready-to-fly
controline models, engines, fuels,
beginner and intermediate level 1 and 2
channel, .049 powered 2-channel ready-to-
fly aircraft; and electric-powered off-road
racing cars and accessories.

FUTABA CORPORATION OF AMERICA
4 Studebaker, Irvine, CA 92718.
Tel: (714) 455-9888.
Products: A complete list of radio control
systems and accessories for aircraft,
helicopter, sailplane, cars and boat
models. Included are the only PCM 1024
systems, electronic speed controls, gyros
and the largest selection of servos. Futaba
also imports YS Futaba engines, Hatori
mufflers, Hirobo planes, the FX10 car and
candy boat.

GREAT PLANES MODEL DIST./KYOSHO
PO Box 4021, Champaign, IL 61820.
Tel: (217) 398-3630.
Products: Distribute most of the hobby
products lines, including proprietary lines
— KYOSHO, O.S., SUPERTIGRE,
IRVINE, HOBBICO, DURATRAX and
GREAT PLANES. Practically any product
in the hobby industry can be found
through Great Planes Model Distributors.

HOBBY DYNAMICS DISTRIBUTORS
PO Box 3726, Champaign, IL 61826-3726.
Tel: (800) 458-0241.
Products: A full service distributor of radio
control hobby products carrying more than
80 lines. Hobby Dynamics is the exclusive
distributor of JR radios and accessories,
Kalt helicopters, Webra engines and
Hirobo cars.

IMEX MODEL CO INC
53 Trade Zone Court, Ronkonkome,
NY 11779.
Tel: (516) 981-2804.
Products: Manufacture radio control car
tyres, rims and accessories.

KO PROPO
Dist. by Global Hobby Distributors,
10725 Ellis Avenue, Fountain Valley
CA 92728-8610.
Tel: (714) 963 0133.
Products: Radio and radio components.

KUSTOM SERVO CORP (ALFA)
11 Columbia Drive, Suite 11, Amherst,
NH 03031.
Tel: (603) 883-3232.
Products: Quality battery chargers, peak
detectors and lightweight battery packs for
electric powered aircraft, airborne
receivers and cars.

MCS PRODUCTS INC
502 Price Drive, Lewisville, TX 75067.
Tel: (214) 463-5864.
Products: Manufacture custom parts, tools
and accessories for 1/10 scale cars, boats
and planes.

MCALLISTER RACING INC
2205 First Street 107, Simi Valley,
CA 93065.
Tel: (805) 583-4473.
Products: Manufacture bodies for 1/10 and
1/12 R/C cars. They have a 1/10 scale
pavement car kit, decals, stripping tape,
and many other accessories for R/C cars.

MCDANIEL R/C INC
12206 Guinevere Road, Glenn Cale,
MD 20769.
Tel: (301) 464-2260.
Products: Manufacture the NI-STARTER,
TORK-STARTER and accessories for
them. They also manufacture electronic
strobes and lights.

MINICRAFT MODELS INC
1510 W 228th Street, Torrance,
CA 90501.
Tel: (213) 775-8836.
Products: Minicraft/Academy radio control
boat and car kits manufactured in Korea
by Academy engineering in USA and
Japan by Minicraft.

MODEL CRAFT MFG
3455 W 8th Street, Los Angeles,
CA 90020-9910.
Tel: (213) 462-2437.
Products: Quality battery chargers for the
modelling industry. Eight available models
to meet everyone's requirements.

MODEL RECTIFIER CORPORATION
(MRC)
200 Carter Drive, Edison, NJ 08817.
Tel: (201) 248-0400.
Products: Exclusive agent for Tamiya R/C
cars, plastic kits and accessories; plus
they import or manufacture R/C gas and
electric airplanes, R/C electric boats,
hobby tools and many different quick
chargers.

NAVCOM INC
350 N Main Street, Huron, OH 44839.
Tel: (419) 433-7626.
Products: Manufacture the Racing Plus
line of DC Ni-Cad battery chargers, the
Racing 12+ charger/discharger, and the
8PDCT Programmable Digital Cell Tester.

NIKKO AMERICA INC
851 International Parkway, Richardson,
TX 75081.
Products: R/C cars, boats, airplanes.

NORCAL AVIONICS
Div A-B Tech Inc, 5689 Glasgow, Troy,
MI 48098.
Tel: (313) 828-8210.
Products: Manufacture digital tachometers,
battery cyclers, battery chargers, digital
meters and all associated accessories.

NOVAK ELECTRONICS
128-C Easy Dyer Road, Santa Ana,
CA 92707.
Tel: (714) 549-3741.
Products: Manufacturers of aftermarket,
high performance electronic equipment for
R/C surface models. Novak's competition
products harnessed to match all major
radio manufacturers include; electronic
speed controls, 2-channel receivers,
battery chargers, high speed servos,
silicone wire and all related accessories.

PARAGON RACING PRODUCTS
690 Industrial Circle South, Shakopee,
MN 55379.
Tel: (612) 496-0091.
Products: Manufactures a wide array of
quality accessories for the serious R/C
enthusiast. Products include motors, tyres,
rims, traction compounds, antennas
lubricants, cleaners, performance parts
and a host of other accessories to make
your racing experience more productive
and enjoyable.

PARMA INTERNATIONAL INC
13927 Progress Parkway, North Royalton,
OH 44133.
Tel: (216) 237-8650.
Products: Electric R/C boats, R/C planes,
R/C cars, and leading manufacturers of
replacement parts and accessories.

POWER MASTER PRODUCTS INC
7807-H Telegraph Road, Montebello,
CA 90640.
Tel: (213) 887-0801.
Products: Manufactures an extensive line
of premium grade model engine fuels from
FA1 to 70% Nitro. Also manufactures
aerosol airplane and electric motor
cleaners, SuperSander and LubeMaster
After Run Oil, Distributes Asano props.

PRO-LINE
PO Box 456, Beaumont, CA 92223.
Tel: (714) 849-9781.
Products: Manufacturers of quality R/C
1/10 scale tyres, wheels, monster truck
conversions, bodies and accessories. New
Red-Race engineered design racing tyres
are the hot ticket. The Pro-Line Pro-Gram
— Product service and support.

PRO-STAR
3615 NW 20th Avenue, Miami, FL 33142.
Products: A full line distributor of R/C
products including Pro-Star chargers, etc.

RACE PREP/AYK RACING
20115 Nordhoff Street, Chatsworth,
CA 91311.
Tel: (818) 341-0842
Products: Race proven by Team Race
Prep. modified and stock motors, 4WD
pro radiant, racing tyres, battery motor
connectors, silicone wire. Exclusive USA.
importer of AYK products.

ROYAL PRODUCTS CORP
790 W Tennessee Avenue, Denver,
CO 80223.
Tel: (303) 778-7711.
Products: Imports a large line of scale
balsa aircraft kits, ARF trainers, ARF sport
aircraft and sailplanes, along with R/C
cars, trucks and motorcycles. Also offers
general R/C accessories from starters to
starting batteries.

SAFT AMERICA INC
711 Industrial Boulevard, Valdosta,
GA 31601. Tel: (912) 247-2331
Products: Manufactures rechargeable Ni-
Cad replacement batteries for VCRs and
camcorders, power tool batteries and Ni-
Cad standard cells in AAA, AA, C, D, and
9 volt sizes.

SKYWARD RESEARCH AND
DEVELOPMENT LABORATORY
4668 Decarie Boulevard, Montreal,
Quebec, H3X 2H5.
Tel: (514) 482-6660.
Products: Radio Control products for
flying, car racing, boating. Manufacture
quality products for the discerning
modeller.

TEAM LOSI INC
1655 E Mission Boulevard, Pomona,
CA 91766.
Tel: (714) 620-0164.
Products: Radio controlled racing cars and
parts. Hand built modified 05 racing
motors, capacity matched Ni-Cad batteries
and precision machine cut gears in 32, 48
and 64 pitch. Vacu-formed Lexan bodies
(painted and clear), and real rubber racing
tyres.

TEKIN ELECTRONICS
970 Calle Negocio, San Clements,
CA 92672
Tel: (714) 498-9518.
Products: Speed controls and accessories.

TEXSON PRECISION PRODUCTS
3615 NW 20th Avenue, Miami, FL 33142.
Tel: (305) 635-3134.
Products: Electronic test equipment,
battery packs, chargers, tools, off-road
cars and accessories, and field boxes.

TRAXXAS
12150 Shiloh Road, Dallas, Texas 75228.
Tel: (214) 613-3300.
Products: Manufactures competition style,
ready-to-run, 1/10 and 1/12 scale electric
R/C cars and boats. All products also
available in kit form. Also manufacture
radio systems, electronic speed controls,
peak chargers and power supplies.

TRINITY PRODUCTS INC
1901 E Linden Avenue 8, Linden,
NJ 07036.
Tel: (201) 862-1705 or (201) 862-1708.
Products: Produce the state-of-the-art
when it comes to motors and batteries for
R/C car racing. Also produce the popular
Speedworks line of R/C car products.
Make virtually every type of accessory
item and import the Schumacher CAT and
TOPCAT.

TWISTER MOTORS
657 E Arrow Highway, Glendora,
CA 91740.
Tel: (818) 914-6177.
Products: Stock and modified motors,
standard and premium matched Sanyo
battery packs and related parts.

UNIVERSAL ENERGY R/C SUPPLIES
130-C East Jefryn Boulevard, Deer Park,
NY 11729.
Tel: (516) 586-9584.
Products: Manufacture battery packs
(standard and customised) and after
market products. Distribute R/C cars,
boats, planes, trains and all related items
such as connectors, chargers, paints etc.

WORLD ENGINES INC
8960 Rossash Avenue, Cincinnati,
OH 45236.
Tel: (513) 793-5900.
Products: Import Brat, ASP, Maloney,
Tactan, Zenoah engines and manufacture
and service Expert radio systems and
accessories. They also have Modeltech
kits.

INDEX

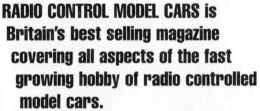